Be Yourself

Living the life you were meant to live by understanding your natural abilities

by John Buffini

OLIVEMOUNT™ PRESS
Carlsbad, CA 92009

BE YOURSELF

Printed in the United States of America

Dedication

To my parents:
who taught us to pursue what
we love and to be ourselves.

Acknowledgements

I've found that people read acknowledgements either to see if they're included or because they wish to glimpse the heart of the author. Because I am synergistic and extremely relational, it is not feasible to thank everyone. This book was not done on a deserted island; it was created with the help of brilliant, synergistic, passionate people, allergic to the mediocre and drawn to the excellent. They surround me with patience and determination and brought home to me how blessed I am. Roxy, there are no words to express the depth of my respect for your love, loyalty, patience and intelligence. You were there for me every step of the way. To the Think Tank, thank you for making this process a fantastic party, and I look forward to our next one. Cynthia, you're the best, most intelligent babysitter I know. I celebrate Valeré for her drive to keep this going and tenacity in not letting me rest. Ty, thank you for bringing creativity and structure to this Nutty Professor. Mort, thanks for making this possible and for keeping my brogue. Gary, you're my satellite perspective. Dermot, you're my passion indicator. Kevin, your insight and humor are equally appreciated. Louise, your loyalty covers the family. Brian, no momentum would be possible without you giving me a jump start. Beverly, for demonstrating that it's okay to be intolerant of mediocrity. Dan, you're a great ambassador of all I know to be true. Kristin, thank you for believing in me. To all my incredible friends who continually refueled me, thank you. This book would not be possible without the vulnerability of my clients, their willingness to share that vulnerability with me, and their willingness to grow. Your growth is my significance. I thank God for not creating a one-size-fits-all set of abilities and for creating us all uniquely.

Contents

"To be nobody-but-yourself—in a world which is doing its best, night and day to make you everybody else— means to fight the hardest battle which any human being can fight; and never stop fighting."

—e.e. cummings

Introduction

One day several summers ago, I was talking on the telephone with a client, reviewing the profile of her natural gifts and abilities. My parents, visiting from Ireland, were sitting on the veranda outside my study. My father is analytical; he spends a lot of time in his head. A few sentences a week is talkative for him. So, as I consulted with my client, I was wondering, "Is my Dad listening? I wonder what he's thinking? And would I ever know?" I finished and hung up the phone.

Sure enough, Dad came in to talk to me about the call, "That was amazing. You really seemed to help that person. You truly seemed to know that person deeply."

This was like manna from heaven for me. I couldn't believe my father said it. But then he asked me a question that to this day makes my heart stand still.

"What would you tell a man who has done the wrong job for 53 years of his life?"

I knew who he meant. He was talking about himself. I couldn't believe it had come out of his mouth. I couldn't believe that after so many years my Dad seemed unaware of who he was or the impact his life had made.

My father has a brilliant mind, yet when he was 12 years old he was yanked out of school and forced to make a living working with his hands. He began by laying terrazzo floors and moved on to house painting which became the family business. He lived in a world where you had to do what you had to do just to survive. My Dad never received a formal education. He always craved it, always missed it, and always insisted that every one of his children have it. Of course, there is nothing undignified about manual labor, but he wanted to be a writer.

It was clear to me from his devastating question that the hardship of his life had caused Dad to lose track of who he was. My father had championed my sister, my brothers and me. He was our first coach. He gave us the clarity and structure that we needed growing up. At the dinner table, he'd stay behind and if any of us wanted to talk, we talked until we were done. His car was called "the Confessional" because you got in, drove around, and poured your heart out to him. Somehow none of this registered with him, at least not at this particular moment, so I took a deep breath and said, "You know what, Dad? You did the wrong job for 53 years of your life. But every night at 5:30 when you got home, you started your real job...drawing out the potential in your kids, coaching us to be the best we could be. Every night at the dinner table you did that. And when you took us out in the car you did that. And now, Dad, because of you and your ways with us, we're going around communicating with people all across the country, encouraging them to be the best they can be."

I'm happy to report that my Dad has finally become aware of his accomplishments. More importantly, he has begun to act on this awareness. Every ten days or so, my brother Brian, the Chairman of the Board of a large business coaching company, gets a call from my father, who maintains the role of insightful advisor and patriarch.

This experience with my Dad serves to reinforce a truth I've discovered from doing thousands of profiles and speaking to thousands of people – most have lost an awareness of who they are. They need to remember. They need to be championed. They need to be seen. This has never been more necessary than now. With the computer, the cellular phone and the palm pilot, our fast-paced generation does not sit around the fireside or the dinner table, reflecting and engaging with one another. We have been given endless opportunities for communication, but technology has taken away the understanding and skill of conversation. Without it, people lack a sense of "true north" in their lives.

Author and poet David Whyte, points out this very lack. In today's society, we've lost the art of conversation...with ourselves, each other and our Creator. Instead of conversing with each other, we talk at each other. The art of conversation has given way to the skill of verbally willing our agenda. Yet, without true conversation, the ability to be seen or to be championed or to remember who we are is effectively lost.

Far too often in my profession, I've seen the unfortunate, sometimes tragic, consequences for people who have not gained an awareness of who they are. On the other hand, I have also witnessed the positive results for people who do become aware of who they are and act on that awareness.

The experience with my Dad served to reinforce my own life purpose. I summarize it as follows: *My purpose on the planet is to empower people to become the best version of them-selves possible by helping them to remember who they are and to act on that awareness.*

When I consult, I usually do it by telephone because my clients are all over the country. I also find that sessions over the phone are more comfortable for my clients. Steve showed up on my radar when my assistant told me that he was determined to do his profile review in person. She spoke with him about the distance and the cost but his mind was set. When he arrived, I understood his insistence on a face-to-face session. It took Steve several minutes to walk down the 50-foot hallway to my conference room. He was a very handsome tri-athlete in his early thirties with a loving wife. Five years before, he had been blessed with the arrival of their son. However, his joy was undermined when Steve was diagnosed with a rare form of ALS. Not much is known about it other than the brain cuts the signal to the muscles. Even though he looked the picture of health, he had difficulty moving and talking.

Steve has a great profile. He is relational, competitive, analytical, big-picture-focused and spontaneous. However, as he watched his child grow, he also saw his own capabilities being eroded by his disease. I am designed to be empathetic, and I was moved by Steve's affliction.

In our session, we strategized about how he could move forward. I pointed out to him that his profile revealed he had a great capacity for knowledge and could gift others with clarity and perspective. He had never really needed to tap into those abilities earlier because his looks, achievements, and Alpha-male persona opened doors for him easily. Now he was being given an opportunity to work smart by leveraging his time, resources and energy. His action steps were to change his job description in the family business, not own his wife's pain, and to ask for help from family and friends when he needs it. He left our session with hope, direction and empowerment.

Steve is an ideal example of the maxim: when we know the truth, it sets us free. He has transformed his life by acting on his newfound awareness; his purpose as a father, husband and professional has been re-established.

One of the most difficult aspects of writing this book is keeping it from becoming just another treatise on self-aware-ness. Self-knowledge is not inherently useful. Self-awareness has to be a pressure point. It must stimulate us to move into the life we're compelled to live. I want this to be a book that makes you aware and provokes you to move, to act and to experience. It is essential to have movement and experiences to celebrate and to inventory them as either substantive mile-stones or islands of remembrance that reinforce the fact that you are alive.

As a profiler, I am fascinated with identical twins and how even with exactly the same DNA and nurturing they can demonstrate such different abilities. The same holds true for families. I have four brothers and a sister. While we have the same genetic make-up and received the same nurture, we are each different. When we gathered around the dinner table for our regular "gab-fest", my father would often comment on how something said could be heard five different ways. Even though my siblings have completely different profiles, they have all excelled in their respective fields by tapping into their own distinctive abilities. The diversity in my family provided the starting point for my own study of individual differences in the gifts and styles of various people. Throughout this book, I share stories from many of my clients (with names and details altered to protect their confidentiality) and from my own family as they have progressed and increasingly embraced the use of their abilities over the years.

Remembering who you are and understanding the subtleties of your design can make the difference between thriving and surviving. Enthusiasm is the key to life. It means "God breathing in our lives". My passion is to help people become aware of who they are innately designed to be, discover their organic essence, and empower them to mirror back their design to their Creator. If I can instruct and inspire you to "wiggle forward," I will have achieved my goal.

CHAPTER 1
YOUR UNIQUE DESIGN

"Every human being is intended to have a character of his own;
to be what no others are, and to do what no other can do."

—William Ellery Channing

You are created with an internal design and an internal
purpose, and these don't change. I believe "You can do anything you put your mind to." However, I don't believe it in the
same way most motivators use it. When you choose to pursue or put your mind to a goal that also matches your heart's
desires, then I believe you can do anything. In other words,
the desires of your heart can be attained because they are
placed there as part of your inborn design. Most of us never
stop to think about where the desires of our hearts come
from, and so many people miss the point of their life. They
don't experience the purpose of their life because they're
going after something they falsely think they should pursue
or some goal their peers are pursuing or some prize of the
moment. When aiming for their life purpose, they miss the
mark because they're pursuing something contrary to their
natural design.

When a large corporation ordered profiles of their candidates for a high-level executive position, the candidates had a lot of incentive to lie in order to gain the large base salary and bonus package. Many of them did lie during their profile interview, attempting to slant the profile results in their favor. Ironically, it didn't matter if they lied. During an interview, we actively listen for the patterns of a person's passion. Their enthusiasm indicates their core natural abilities, and it is difficult to fake it. For example, if the candidates lied about being self-starters, their voice trailed off as they talked about it because their passion was actually in finishing or maintaining a project given to them. Your design isn't what you try to be; it's who you are! Many people think that their frame of mind has to be "just right" when interviewed for their profile assessment. But people always leak who they are.

When speaking of abilities, I am talking about you – the unique you. I've reviewed the profiles of thousands of individuals from all over...corporate executives, teenagers, homemakers, millionaires, and people who are barely getting by. And I have never seen two profiles exactly alike. That is not surprising. Just as each of us has a unique fingerprint and a face peculiarly our own that greets us in our bathroom mirror every morning, we have an internal design that is unique.

Because everyone leaks who they are, it is possible to learn what to look for to capture who a person is. Using observational analysis, we evaluate an individual's patterns of gifts, abilities and styles. Based on this profile, we instruct the individual as to how this pattern of abilities can be used in a wonderfully dynamic way. Observational analysis has been utilized for as long as men and women have been aware of differences between individuals. The Greeks, the Sufis and many other cultures used it. I have refined the technique and applied it to the problems individuals face in the 21st century.

Your design is comprised of your innate abilities, what you gravitate to naturally. Everyone in my large family is right-handed. When my third nephew was born, we noticed early on that he preferred to use his left hand. He was naturally adept at using it. We tested his determination to be left-handed by putting items into his right hand. Time after time, he'd switch them to his dominant hand. It wasn't heredity nor was it his nurture. He was simply innately compelled to use his left hand. Similarly, we are naturally compelled to use certain attributes irrespective of our nurture or genetics.

For many of us, one of our earliest experiments from science class was observing the consistency of a compass pointing north. No matter how much the needle is deterred from its purpose, nothing will wear down its resolve to find north. Likewise, on our journey in life we are designed to find our own true north. We may be deterred or detoured, but we remain in a state of internal awareness as to whether or not we are pursuing our true purpose. That innate awareness orients us to our personal true north. It's a compulsion to move toward what we are designed to do.

If you're not aware of what your innate and learned abilities are, however, you do not know what your true north is. You don't know whether you're moving toward success, significance and thriving or toward atrophy, loss and surviving. You may be giving your power away to other people, trying to find yourself in their eyes, to find your validation in their expectations and their approval. That is a goal, but perhaps it doesn't answer why you were put on this planet.

As I've already mentioned, your innate abilities are demonstrated by your enthusiasm. Enthusiasm comes from the word "in-Theo" which means "God-sized fullness". There is no more passionate a word than enthusiasm. You don't register enthusiasm by focusing on what's wrong with you but by concentrating on what is right about you and folding that into your life, your business and your relationships. Enthusiasm literally inoculates you against burnout.

Innate Abilities vs. Learned Abilities. Webster's New Collegiate Dictionary defines the word *ability* as "the quality or state of being able, competence in doing, or skill". This dictionary defines *learn* as, "to gain knowledge or understanding or skill in by study, instruction or experience; to come to be able". We can have abilities from birth or we can learn them.

Innate abilities are not learned. They are inborn. They come naturally and unconsciously to you. Your innate abilities are your natural gifts and they reveal truths about you. They are basic to who you are, and they make you come to life. They are what you are passionate about, and they show up whether you are 5, 25 or 55 years old. Natural abilities must be cultivated, fostered and nurtured; not ignored, abandoned, and orphaned.

Learned abilities are tasks, skills, and behavioral tendencies that you acquire. A learned ability is a result of nurture and experience. What you learn depends on your environment, what's expected of you, your culture. Your learned abilities are secondary to your innate abilities.

> **When you practice looking into your own motivation, you're well on your way to understanding yourself and others.**

This point can be confusing, so a few examples may clarify it. If one of your innate abilities is a strong competitive drive, how your competitiveness plays itself out can vary, and this depends on your nurture. If you grew up in a family that loved to play sports and your parents signed you up for tennis lessons, your competitive drive might be expressed by being on the tennis team at school. However, if your family emphasized music, you might learn to play the piano because your mother wanted you to. Then you might express your competitive drive through piano competitions. The learned ability is piano or tennis, but your innate ability is competing.

Another example is someone whose innate ability is to impact the lives of others. If the individual's parents were teachers who encouraged their child to become a teacher, teaching might be the way this primary or innate ability played out. If one of the parents was a politician or an actor, the child might be encouraged to develop the skills needed for politics or acting. Of paramount importance to the individual is not the career in teaching or politics or acting, but the opportunity to impact the lives of others. That is what engages their passion and makes life rewarding.

Recognizing the passion behind the pursuit. This is key to distinguishing between learned and innate abilities. My family members are all sports enthusiasts. And, they actively participate in many sports. So when I train for a marathon with them or play a round of golf, it is because I'm a sports enthusiast too, right?! Wrong! I am by nature the reader, the season ticket holder at the theater, the one who appreciates art. I have the ability to appreciate the beauty in the arts and in life, but I also have abilities that are relational. Therefore, I participate as a "team player" when I play sports because I enjoy the friendly camaraderie of a golf scramble, and I enjoy the connection to others I feel when I compete in a race. On the surface you see me as a sports enthusiast, but it's misleading.

I have friends who are well-known for their artistic endeavors. Their four children are artistic and not athletic. However, if you look behind the initial impression, you will find that one child likes to create private introspective moments with his music; another loves music competitions; the third wants to be provocative and liked with his art; the fourth wants to convey serious or inspirational thought to his audience. When you practice looking into your own motivation, you're well on your way to understanding yourself and others.

Some learned abilities are skills essential for survival, emotionally and physically. Your learned abilities enable you to navigate through life, but they don't necessarily have anything to do with your thriving. In order to thrive, you have to engage your innate abilities.

Furthermore, it is the blending of your learned abilities with your innate abilities that's crucial to experiencing success and significance...thriving, rather than just surviving. Pavarotti has a natural ability to sing and a wonderful instrument, his voice. Through exceptional discipline and practice, he has learned the necessary skills. However, without his passion, without his zeal for excellence and his desire to move his audience, he would technically sing well, but would not thrive the way he obviously does.

Your profile doesn't pigeonhole you or determine your job destiny. Instead of limiting you, it opens up the many possibilities available to you, based on your multi-faceted design. Even for someone like Prince William, who was born with a predetermined job description, his natural abilities will shape how he'll fulfill the role of king. William was not born with the innate abilities needed to be King of England. Some of his natural abilities have leaked out: to nurture and care for people, to enjoy competition, to value camaraderie. His innate abilities will surface, even inside his future formal role as king.

My brother Brian sold real estate with great success. He now has a national company that coaches people to be successful in their own businesses. Many of them are realtors. I provide profiles for them, and I am fascinated by the broad variety of people drawn to this field. Nurturers are attracted to selling real estate because they like to help others find a home. Free-spirited people come to it because of the freedom and flexibility the industry provides. Some are drawn to this profession because they love the negotiations and the daily challenges. Their profiles do not narrowly define the specific job they should go into. Rather, the profiles reveal the variety of jobs they can do and indicate how people with varied profiles can do the same job differently, according to their own style.

I've sought to correct elements of past profiling systems that put people into one of 32 categories or into a combination of these categories. I also believe that it is wrong to compare individuals on a scale with everyone who took a similar test. These approaches limit results. They put a person in a box. There are only 32 YESes or boxes you can be put into, but there are an infinite number of NOs. My technique, the Ability Management Profile, is designed to look for the YESes rather than the NOs. My goal is to celebrate the unique gifts of the individual. You are compared to no one. My idea is not to limit or label you. My focus is to provide you a tool that opens up a conversation on how to empower you. I seek to have you understand and embrace your innate gifts and learn how to manage them.

Many of us have been told that if we focus on fixing what is wrong with us, we will right ourselves. Using your Ability Management Profile, we focus on what is right with you.

Mediocrity is established when we focus on our weaknesses. Success and significance are manifested when we focus on our strengths and create a mechanism to support our weaknesses.

While providing an atmosphere of acceptance and grace, I challenge people with the truth about themselves, emphasizing what is right about them, not what's wrong. You've heard many times, "work on your weaknesses." Why? So you can become mediocre? My work is to help you harness what you're good at and delegate what you're not good at.

Your abilities interact in combination to shape who you are designed to be. An important aspect of using your abilities, styles and perspectives optimally is in the interplay...in how these areas complement each other, intensify each other, or cause you internal conflict. When I go over a person's profile with them, I want to shed light on the joys and frustrations of being that individual. When one ability interacts with another, both combine to form a hybrid. For example, if the Romantic attribute interacts with an attribute that loves to learn and explore, it might prompt the individual to work as a forest ranger. If the Romantic attribute is combined with the love of improving and refining things, the individual might be an interior designer.

How you use your natural abilities is as important as the particular abilities you have to use. Your styles represent the ways in which you use your unique abilities. This is about how you work, how you parent, and how you relate to others. It's about the environment for you to thrive, the best environment for you to learn and grow toward success and significance. With regard to styles, we talk about how you naturally communicate; how you need to be communicated with; where your significance stems from. With regard to time, we look at several areas: What is your reality? What are you aware of? What do you focus on? How do you move through time? Quickly? Slowly? The big question is: How can your natural styles optimally benefit your life? I hope and expect that this book will be a beginning for you to discover answers for yourself.

Overview of Profile Elements

REPRESENTATIVE ATTRIBUTES	STYLES	TIME
Abstract Family Artist **Discern Family** Refiner	**WORK STYLE:** MOTIVATOR FACILITATOR STRATEGIST	**ENERGY:** CATALYTIC FINITE PERIODIC PERPETUAL
Growth Family Pioneer **Impress Family** Performer **Intense Competitor Family** Olympian	**OPTIMAL LEARNING ENVIRONMENT:** ANALYTICAL INDEPENDENT KINESTHETIC SYNERGISTIC	**PERFORMANCE:** CREATE-EXECUTE CREATE-FINALIZE EXECUTE-FINALIZE EXECUTE-SUPPORT
Intense Freedom Family Free Spirit **Intense Integrity Family** Justice	**CORE NATURE:** AESTHETIC PRAGMATIC	**RHYTHM:** METICULOUS TEMPERATE RAPID
Learn Family Scholar **Relational Family** Nurturer **Structure Family** Engineer	**SIGNIFICANT SOCIAL ENVIRONMENT:** INTROSPECTIVE INTROSPECTIVE-RELATIONAL GREGARIOUS	**FOCUS:** SPECIFIC SPECTRUM GLOBAL

CHAPTER 2
WHO ARE YOU?

"Each of us has some unique capability waiting for realization. Every person is valuable in his own existence, for himself alone...each of us can bring to fruition these innate, God-given abilities."

—George H. Bender

The more gadgets we have to help us save time, the more we try to do. As we rush from one task to the next, we tend to forget who we are. The demands and entertainments of our digital society carry us away from ourselves. In our haste, we've mislaid the ability to hold a conversation with ourselves, with each other and with our Creator. Remembering who you are is essential to opening those conversations.

Think about your innate abilities. They are like breathing...intricate, complicated...but we do it automatically without thinking about it. Listen to how you "breathe" and what you're naturally designed to do. Few of us spend time considering what we do naturally. Very few focus on being right-handed . . .unless they lose their right hand. It slips under their radar. It's a built-in ability. But those who are left-handed pay attention to it. They become aware of right-handed scissors and where they sit at a table. Being left-handed goes against the majority.

People tend to focus on what they don't do naturally. Most are not aware of their own natural abilities, and so they don't appreciate them. Instead, they often apologize for who they are. Becoming aware requires you to remember who you are and allows you to appreciate your own unique design. It also gives you an appreciation for the unique designs of others.

Awareness of differences in natural abilities promotes empathy rather than judging. When people assume that everyone has the same abilities they have, it can result in judgment and conflict. For example, Bob might be Global, someone who focuses on the big picture, and also Meticulous, someone who processes deliberately. A person without that combination of abilities might judge Bob as being lazy or disengaged from the present. Kathy, who is Specific, focusing on the present, and Finite, always acting with the end in mind, can be perceived as moody and abrupt by someone who doesn't share her abilities. Now picture Bob and Kathy as a couple. It doesn't take much to imagine the sparks flying in that house and how they would wear each other down trying to change each other.

While growing up, some of you had family and friends who judged you in the same way. A friend of mine is a per-former. He has no problem performing in front of thousands, yet he is painfully shy about calling people on the phone. His family saw him as irresponsible and unsociable. Another friend has an incredible eye for antiques; her collection is remarkable. She knows all the details about what to collect and the value, but she can't balance her checkbook. Her father regarded her as stupid. Another of my friends makes independent films. He is very creative, bright and witty, and he was shocked to learn that most people do not naturally see what he sees. Becoming aware of the unique differences in people had great value for him, he told me. It permitted him to have patience with others where he wasn't naturally designed to be patient.

The reality is that no one has it all. Each of us is brilliant at some things and inept at others. That alone is cause for accurate humility. It is the reason we need one another, to appreciate those who have gifts that differ from ours.

We can regard someone with a natural style different from ours as a predator to our innate abilities. They bring questions to mind: "Will he slow me down? Will she compromise my excellence? Will he undermine my impact?"

From there, we might establish a position of defensiveness or hostility. A much better approach is to celebrate or leverage the natural abilities of the other individual. Find out what they have to offer and tap into those areas.

Let me point out that a predator, as I use the term, is anything that preys on, destroys or corrodes the true nature of an ability. Like a predatory animal triggering basic fear within its prey, it freezes that ability. It can roar or whisper and often represents the worst fear of that ability.

Your natural abilities can be a blessing or a curse, depending on how you use them. Think of your abilities as a knife. If you use it to cut your meat, you're using it correctly. If you use it inappropriately and poke yourself in the eye or cut yourself, the knife causes you pain. You don't want to use it anymore! If you have a sufficiently bad experience using one of your abilities, you tend to set that natural gift aside out of frustration or fear. This may cause you great internal conflict: you want to experience the rewards of using your gift properly; at the same time you don't want the pain caused when you misuse that ability. Just because something comes naturally to us, that does not mean it will manage itself. Instead, it requires that we consciously choose to manage the ability. We have to learn when to use the gas and when to brake.

Leaning into your abilities. We break through mediocrity toward success when we lean into what our natural profile compels us to do. Success and significance are established when we focus on our strengths. There is an old saying, "When you drill for water, don't dig ten six-foot wells. Dig one sixty-foot well!" Life is much more meaningful when you consciously move toward mastery of your abilities. When you lean into your design, it creates confidence and competence.

Mirroring back your creation to your Creator. I was reviewing the profile of a man who has three Ph.D.

degrees, and he commented to me, "When you talk about these abilities and brilliance, you are actually talking about *potential brilliance*, right?"

This is an important point and valid observation. These are your innate abilities. They are organic. If you don't set up a greenhouse with the right environment, fertilizer, watering schedule and nutrients...everything needed to grow that organic ability...your natural internal design will not be moved toward brilliance. *Your abilities are your potential brilliance.* I have done profiles for people with dramatic abilities which they have not chosen to harness, leverage, celebrate, champion or cultivate. They are burying their talents and gifts in the ground.

Let me repeat something I said at the beginning. It is a vital point. Becoming self-aware is not necessarily useful in itself. Self-awareness has to be a pressure point. It must stimulate us to move inside the life we are compelled to live. I want this book to make you aware and provoke you to move, to act and to experience.

We must move forward, have experiences to celebrate and to inventory as either substantive milestones or islands of remembrance that reinforce the fact we are alive.

What I don't wish to do is to help you create an abstract universe of self-discovery. I do want you to become aware of who you are in terms of your innate design and to ultimately mirror back your creation to your Creator. You accomplish this through movement, appreciation and obedience to who you are designed to be. Ironically, many people I profile shake their fists at the heavens looking for a manufacturer's rebate. Your Creator doesn't make mistakes!

The key is to enthusiastically pursue your life desires, the desires of your heart. That movement is where you're meant to find yourself. Homemaker, artist, teacher, or industry leader...whatever your pursuit, it is irrelevant as long as you are doing what you were put on this planet to do. I want self-awareness to be the personal, positive pressure point that gets you to move toward the success and significance you've been created for.

Learning to thrive. It's about more than just surviving. No matter how difficult your current circumstances, you can wiggle forward. At my church in Southern California one Sunday, a petite teenager stood up behind the massive pulpit to share her story with us. She was seventeen and had emancipated herself two years earlier from her addicted, abusive mother. She had never met her father. Despite the adversity, the girl had persevered with high school. Because a kind couple opened their home to her, she had gained some measure of stability in her life. She became an expert marksman in school, and the Army gave her a scholarship to attend Officer's Training. I was so moved by her story that I offered to profile her. It turned out I was the one who was blessed when I consulted with her. She was realistic about her history and had chosen not to become a victim of it. Instead, her adversity fueled her to become focused, move forward, and to celebrate her achievements. She had great expectations for her life. Even if she does not hit her targets with 100% accuracy, I am certain that significance and thriving are assured for her.

Abuse of abilities. I am aware that, as a family, we Buffinis are unusual. My brothers and I impact thousands of people across the country. We are truly blessed to be doing what we are doing. Maybe because we are "the Osmonds of personal development," we attract many people who are hungry for what we have as a family. This was brought home for me when a woman who was signing up for personal coaching said, "Here are my adoption papers into the Buffini family."

Perhaps our old-world perspective is part of it, but I believe people see us as an effective family, mysteriously working well together...and for many it points up a lack in their own lives. Unfortunately, a great number of people grew up in families that did not champion them, that did not encourage them to use their natural abilities. I've talked to many whose families either ignored what they had to offer or wanted them to change somehow. As adults, we can continue to abuse our natural abilities through neglect or embarrassment, maybe because we are not championed to use them. We may also abuse them by using only those abilities we are celebrated for and ignoring or neglecting the others. The result is that we become caricatures of our true selves.

Environment is important. Fear; family, social and institutional taboos; missed opportunities; shut-down: we have all experienced these at some point. When we find ourselves in an environment too harsh for our natural abilities to thrive, then we are like orchids in the desert. Orchids require a greenhouse with just the right soil, fertilizer, light, temperature and humidity. Our life circumstances can break the greenhouse glass and let in cold, dry air that robs us of what is essential to us.

I help my clients create an environment for their humanity by helping them become aware of their own organic abilities and what they need to perform optimally. The proper environment lets you use your abilities to the fullest, so you can move towards a thriving, significant life.

Avoiding use of an ability or style. When it comes to self, many of us tend to react punitively to our life circumstances. Our internal dialogue might be, "I'm in debt, so I'll stop having fun." or "I made some mistakes years ago, and I won't forgive myself."

One of my clients has a highly competitive ability in his profile. Years ago, he was an Olympic hopeful, but he had to pass up the opportunity to be on the team. He had to work to support his mother and sister, and he had no time to train. He succumbed to loss and bitterness and went on for the next eleven years, suppressing his desire to compete in his chosen sport. His enthusiasm for life suffered. His "I could have been a contender" attitude wore thin on those around him, and he withdrew from family and friends. I worked on helping him to forgive himself and to let go of the past. I directed his attention into the precious present and onto how he could re-awaken his competitive abilities and use them to move toward thriving. Today, he coaches a college athletic team, and he is being celebrated for using his tenure, expertise and innate abilities. He has experienced exponential growth in other areas and has reclaimed his life.

It's never too late to grow into who you are. However, because of fatigue, hopelessness or bitterness, some people give themselves over to an apathetic existence. I was approached by a woman to help her elderly parents. She expressed hope that the compassion and truth I'd shared with her could help her mother and father enjoy their remaining years. Fred and Molly had grown up during the depression and the austerity of that environment had shaped them by triggering a life-long fear of loss. In the ensuing decades, they had moved to Florida and amassed a large fortune. Neither the sunshine of that state nor their wealth made much impact on their daily lives. They always appeared to be sad and fearful. They could have lived in luxury for the rest of their lives without making a dent in their fortune. The tragedy was that they lived as a paralyzed couple; anxious and fretful about today and terrified about tomorrow. Their four adult children tried everything to enliven them, but to no avail. It quickly became apparent to me that their power had been lost in the depression. These otherwise smart people had chosen to hold life at arm's length. They'd decided to distrust anything outside of their known world. In a sense, they volunteered to be stranded on an island of NO surrounded by a sea of YESes.

Their children were their world; they'd created a stable loving environment for them, which unfortunately was anchored by fear. The children each married very different persons, but ironically their spouses have one characteristic in common: they love to live, be it traveling the world or experiencing the best life has to offer. The four children have little interaction with their parents because their joy is stolen if they're around their parents for long. To escape that, they've each moved thousands of miles away. And so, this rich couple with their poor lives had their world become even more lonely and entrenched. When I talked with them, I reminded them that they had all the resources they could possibly need. I was the ambassador of possibilities and YESes, and I represented a threat to their world. Even though they heard the truth about themselves, they wouldn't act on the insights I shared. Although gentle in their demeanor, they resolutely held onto their known stability and rejected any new hope that was offered. Even though it saddens my heart when I think of them, I am grateful to have met them because they are a reminder to live life with vigilance to one's own condition. Irrespective of their circumstances, everyone has an opportunity to wiggle forward in life. Those who do not seize the opportunity do themselves disservice and harm.

Overuse of an ability or style. There is a decidedly negative effect if you overuse one ability at the expense of your other natural abilities. Often, those people who are celebrated for being quick-witted and funny are unfulfilled because they are *only* celebrated for those abilities. They feel a vacuum of significance, and this may precipitate self-destructive behavior. If we're to establish a balanced or whole-view approach to significance in the major areas of life, we need to manage, cultivate, and nurture the time, resources and energy required to realize our dreams, visions and aspirations.

PEOPLE DON'T CHANGE. They can become a better version of who they are or a bent-and-broken version of who they are.

Using your abilities is as natural as breathing, but managing them requires far more finesse. I have an attribute I share with a good friend of mine I'll call Tony: it is to refine and improve people, organizations and things. In the right circumstances, this ability is extremely valuable, insightful and appreciated. In the wrong circumstances, it can be destructive. Tony's wife is athletic and their children are gifted athletes. Tony delights in the athletic excellence of his children...so much that his Refiner attribute is prompted to improve their natural abilities. He can easily slip from insightful coach to tyrannical father. Awareness of this zealous overuse of his natural gift can make all the difference between being remembered as a champion by his kids or as a negative critic. Remember, when unmanaged, our greatest gifts are our greatest disabilities.

Awareness that people don't change. This is where I differ with those in the self-improvement community. We do not change fundamentally. The truth about you remains consistent whether you are 5, 25 or 55 years old. We have a choice to become a better version or a bent-and-broken version of our current self. I strongly disagree with the "blank-slate" philosophy. I am concerned that we get off to a bad start if we try to ignore or reinvent our core nature. That's wishing ourselves away. When it comes to assessing who we are, it's not realistic to begin the process by wishing away any part of ourselves or our nurture. If you're an orchid in the desert, wishing to be a cactus is futile.

We talk about opposites attracting. I believe that individuals are drawn to the strengths they see in another person, the abilities they themselves do not innately possess. The odd thing is that once they get into a partnership or committed relationship they then try to change the other person. It never ceases to amaze me when I see the tenacity and determination of such couples to wear each other down. Each is bent to get their partner to embrace their agenda and see things their way.

One of the great fallacies in relationships is that we think we can change the other person. We wrongly believe that if we just keep working at it, we can get the other person to change by wearing them down. I met a couple who'd been married 44 years and they were still trying to change each other! The years of wasted energy, frustration and hopelessness are inconsequential to them because wearing their partner down takes precedence. Relationships require perspective, strategy and vulnerability. They also require knowing who you are and finding out with whom you are in a relationship.

And here's the revelation I share with folks across the country: PEOPLE DON'T CHANGE. They can become a better version of who they are or a bent-and-broken version of who they are. When individuals are in survival mode, we often find that they have transformed into the bent-and-broken version. When people remember who they are and lean into their abilities, it is usually because they have leveraged their innate gifts to highest and best use in their environment.

Unused abilities don't die. They languish in a kind of hell. Again, everybody has an internal monologue. Think of your subconscious as a supercomputer without a sense of humor. It processes all day and dreams all night. If some of your innate abilities are not activated, they report their pain to your subconscious every day of every week of every month of every year. The ability doesn't die. It withers; it groans; it is miserable and oppressed. It incubates this hunger that we project onto others. We quietly hope that someone will rescue us from that natural longing or unused ability inside us. In that hope, we unconsciously set up our relationships to disappoint us, hurt us and wound us.

I tell my clients, "Think of your abilities as the white Arabian stallions in Ben Hur. They're magnificent, intense, glorious. But they have to be deftly managed so that they can make the corners in life's race. At other times, joyously, the reins can be let go to permit the stallions to run free. Also, the horses must be teamed in the right order and actively moving in the same direction; not one horse taking the rest of the team off-course."

Taking your innate abilities from the subconscious to the conscious is the beginning of managing your abilities. The next step is learning how to identify and inventory your innate abilities.

CHAPTER 3
TAKING INVENTORY OF
YOUR INNATE ABILITIES

"Too many people overvalue what they are not and undervalue what they are."

—Malcolm Forbes

When we profile you, we're searching for your dominant innate abilities. We filter through the conversation to also establish the ways you naturally work, learn, and communicate; what your core nature is; and the best environment for you to thrive. We try to find out what rewards and motivates you. We also look for the way you interact with time. How do you move through time...quickly or slowly? What is your focus? Do you tend to look immediately in front of you or out into the future? What are you conscious of in regard to time? Do you see natural breaks or is it continuous? All these things contribute to your recognizable internal design.

Specific Abilities. The first area we assess is your dominant attributes or abilities. We've grouped all abilities into ten families of similar abilities. Because of the large number of abilities possible, rather than burden you with encyclopedic information on all of them, I have chosen to present a representative ability from each family.

FAMILIES OF ABILITIES

Abstract Family	Intense Integrity Family
Discern Family	Impress Family
Growth Family	Learn Family
Intense Competitor Family	Relational Family
Intense Freedom Family	Structure Family

In subsequent chapters, we isolate, describe and discuss each ability. How a specific ability interacts with other abilities contributes to your uniqueness. It also adds to the blending of the characteristics, similar to the effect achieved when you mix two or more colors to get a third distinct color. Some profile systems over-simplify our complex designs by putting us into restrictive categories when actually we are each individual diamonds with different cuts, colors, clarities and carat weights. The Ability Management personal profiling process in a sense cuts away at the raw diamond to get to the true facets of who you are.

This book is written for a broad audience, and it is not possible to be as thorough as the discovery process we provide when doing individual profiles. However, it will introduce you to the process and provide insights into your profile that you will be able to use in your personal and professional life. As you read over the description of each representative ability, be on the lookout for those which touch your passion – the abilities that resonate with you, that get you excited. If you find yourself identifying with all of them, it's going to confuse you...like the medical student who thought he had every disease he studied. This can happen because you can find part of every ability in yourself. Again, you're looking for your dominant abilities, those with which you feel the strongest identification.

An alternative way to identify a dominant ability is by the pain or trouble associated with it. Attributes can hinder as well as help, and you may have noted this hindrance with a particular attribute. A good way to validate your findings is to check them out with people you trust and who know you well. Also check against your personal history. Everyone knows instances of how they have or haven't used their abilities, and how their nurture has championed or oppressed them. Everyone has stories about these things that affect them.

However, somewhere along the way, people all have an opportunity to leak who they are and to reflect on that. My expectation in communicating this process *is not that you will fully see yourself*, but that you will be able to:

❑ clearly identify those abilities that most represent you, how they can benefit you and how they can get you into trouble;

❑ apply your new awareness to create the actions, life experiences, and results you are designed to experience;

❑ start taking the action necessary for movement toward success and significance in your life.

We will discuss how to inventory and manage your movements so that you are not free-falling your way to success and significance; that is as absurd as it sounds. Instead, with better perspective, you'll be able to strategically move through the roadblocks of your life.

Now let's discuss what's in your toolbox. We're all made in God's image…a very full picture…so we all come with a complete set of tools. On the top layer of our toolbox are the tools we tend to use most, right at our fingertips, so to speak. These are our *dominant* abilities. The tools further down in our toolbox are available to us when we need them, but we have to dig further to get them. A dramatic example is the mother who finds the strength to lift the car off her child. In a crisis, she employs the Olympian ability. It might be the only time in her life she uses it. The drive to overcome challenges may not be among her dominant attributes, but at that moment of crisis, she reaches further into her Creator-inspired toolbox to grab the right tool.

Let's begin our survey with Nurturer from the Relational Family, a marvelous tool.

CHAPTER 4
NURTURER
from the Relational Family

"What do we live for if not to make life less difficult for each other?"

—George Eliot

A Nurturer values people before anything else. A Nurturer knows what to say to someone who is experiencing difficult times. It is the person most likely to end up with a date by the end of the night or the one you would most like to deal with at the DMV. Nurturers value people by listening, helping and cherishing them. They make it look effortless because they enjoy doing these things.

In some families, one member is regarded as the glue. That person values the other members of the family by putting them first, before everything else, no matter what. Nurturers are always aware of the heartbeat behind any project. They all have an unusually high level of empathy for others; that's why people come to them with personal issues. Nurturers get their significance from realizing the impact they have on the lives of others. They're at their best when involved in relationships that deserve them and when they find the balance between giving care and receiving it. Others trust their sincerity and attention.

Carol is excellent at using her Nurturer ability. In her role as a business coach, this ability enables her to change a person's attitude or perspective for the long term. Her opinions and input are respected and acted upon. She's not afraid to tell people the hard truth if she believes they will benefit from it. Since her job is people-intensive, it is important for her to take care of herself emotionally as well as physically. In the past few years, she has learned to get massages, work out at the gym, and take time for dinner and a play or movie with friends, all on a regular basis. She has learned to balance the demands of her Nurturer ability with the need to take care of herself.

Mother Teresa is a supreme example of someone who cared deeply for others. This saintly woman was an ambassador for dynamically nurturing others. Like many Nurturers, she had a hard time receiving. It's easy for Nurturers to put their own needs on hold because of a wonderful desire to help others. At times, Mother Teresa would not take her medications or wouldn't rest. Consequently, her support team had to stop what they were doing to care for her. As a Nurturer, it is natural for you to gift others with Nurture, but make sure you also receive the gift of nurture from others.

For myself, growing up in Ireland, as a Nurturer I wanted to help others in a significant way. However, I was terrified that I would lose myself in it and end up living in dire poverty. No one can volunteer to nurture at the complete abandonment of their own humanity. If you have a Relational ability, as you care for others, first take care of yourself so you don't become susceptible to disillusionment and burnout. It takes the pressure off! If you know how to rejuvenate yourself regularly, you're better able to nurture others.

Needs: God-sized and me-sized. In Ireland, the pace of our lives was different than in America. Having lived the past 16 years in the U.S., my perspectives remain somewhat different. Whenever I was feeling depressed, put upon, or unappreciated, my Mom used to say to me, "Get off the cross. We need the wood." I've held onto that wonderful word-picture because it reminds me that:

❏ I'm not a deity. There are me-sized needs on my conveyor belt and there are God-sized needs. Differentiating between them is essential. You have to be able to walk away from the needs you're not designed for and accept those you are supposed to.

❏ Three rules apply to relationships. God uses these rules in His relationship with us. We need to do the same in our relationships with others.
  1. Respect the person's dignity.
  2. Have the grace to accept, not necessarily agree with, the person's choices or decisions.
  3. Allow the person to experience the consequences of their decisions.

The third rule is difficult for a Nurturer to follow naturally. Nurturers can miss the mark in a relationship because it pains them to see human suffering. My favorite writer, C.S. Lewis said, "Pain is God's megaphone to the world." That is how He gets our attention. When a person comes to the end of self, that's where God is. That's where pain and clarity come in. What people do with that painful clarity can move them toward the success and significance they're designed for. Nurturers tend to become human trampolines if they let us bounce our problems off them without letting us come to the end of ourselves. Sometimes it's necessary to stand back and let the person you care about experience the pain in order for them to gain the clarity.

Nurturers must be in relationships that deserve them. They must qualify their personal and professional relationships, based not on ego but on reciprocity. They would do themselves a favor by asking, "Who gets to have me? As I give the very best of myself, how does this individual, institution or organization reciprocate?"

Personally, I have a busy travel schedule. There are a lot of things going on in my day, in my world, in my week. I had a friend who constantly asked me to do him favors because he and his wife traveled a lot. Would I mind taking them to the airport? Would I mind watching the dog, getting the mail, making sure the lawn was watered? They lived nine miles from me, and the airport was 35 miles away. After years of favors, on the long drive back from taking them to the airport one night, I asked myself, "What was my true motivation for helping him?" It was to be liked and accepted. After some serious soul searching, I stopped those behaviors and the relationship dissolved. I was surprised to discover the extra time I had to devote to my true purpose – helping other people find themselves.

On the conveyor belt of life as it passes moment by moment, there are the needs of your spouse, children, parents, colleagues, clients...even the dog. Nurturers tend to put them all ahead of their own needs. They do so in the hope that their own unspoken needs will eventually be met. They have a difficult time prioritizing their own needs and, as a consequence, frequently their needs go unmet.

Nurturers are the Marcel Marceaus of relationships. They do not naturally articulate their wants. In personal and professional relationships, Nurturers set themselves up for disappointment by not expressing their needs, assuming that others are empathetic enough to recognize them and reciprocate. Their silence usually communicates to others that they are fine and satisfied. It can communicate everything but the truth. Nurturers need to participate in the dance of their relationships. They need to *practice* articulating their needs, desires and frustrations.

I often give this homework assignment to Nurturers: write down everything you don't want personally and professionally. When you're satisfied with that list, go back and find the WANT that is inside each DON'T WANT. These are what we call "filters". Once you have established your DON'T WANTS and have clarified your WANTS, then you can ask yourself another filter question: What time, resources and energy are required to manifest those wants in my life?

The second most difficult act for a Nurturer after articulating a want is to stand back and receive. If there is no reciprocity and nothing is received, perhaps it shows the non-reciprocator has nothing to give in the relationship.

Remember, "Your friends are the family you choose." I am talking here to people with a relational attribute, those who are other-people focused and giving in nature. If you are a natural giver, you need to make sure you are receiving. It refuels your relational gas tank.

You can work with orphans and get great satisfaction from it. However, you also need relationships with people who watch out for you, make sure you are taking care of yourself, and are genuinely concerned for your emotional, physical, and environmental well-being. In your key relationships, you need reciprocity.

CHAPTER 5
JUSTICE
from the Intense Integrity Family

"Integrity simply means a willingness not to violate one's identity."
—Erich Fromm

There is nobility in truth and in those who hunt for it and insist upon it. Justices are our human compasses. They point us to true north and keep us from straying off course. You see this in the judge, lawyer or politician who won't sell out and chooses the right way. What would happen in our legal, financial or spiritual worlds if no one had these Integrity attributes? Where would excellence be if we had no one to establish or maintain standards? Do you value people who tell you the truth? Do you appreciate people with strong follow-through? Do you value people who take things seriously? Justices go right to the bottom line.

My brother Gary has earned the nickname Mr. Integrity. We go to him to sort out the blurred boundaries and the gray areas of tough situations. He gives us a clear sense of direction and a model of the truth. It is reassuring and motivating to have a Justice help you sort out what's real and true.

Justices are always seeking to apply their deeply-held values, principles and convictions to life. And the Justice attribute can show up in diverse ways. It was easy to share with a minister how his Integrity attribute showed up in his ministry. However, the next day, I was talking with a client, an exotic dancer from Las Vegas, discussing her Integrity ability. She believed without doubt that she helped marriages stay together because she provided a service and a release to sexually frustrated men. They returned to their wives feeling better. After my initial dismay, I realized she was trying to process her world through her Integrity ability. Integrity can be manifested in traditional or non-traditional ways. Justices have to match who they are with what they do. They have to ground themselves in truth.

Martin Luther King's values, principles and convictions helped change the law, the world and history for the better. His determination forced a generation to react positively to the truths he saw. It is our loss that he couldn't be convinced to change his security and accessibility with regard to the growing threats against his life.

The gift of a Justice is to firmly hold the truth dear. The flipside is that they can stubbornly hold onto distorted truths. I believe Hitler was convinced he was right and took that belief with him to the grave. I doubt he realized the madness of his distortions that scarred generations and cataclysmically impacted history. Thankfully, Justices rarely hold bent truths as globally destructive. However, they can hold distorted truths that may be harmful to their own lives.

The process is both subtle and insidious. From their historic nurture or authority figures, Justices can get the notion that there is something wrong with them or that they need to be more like a sibling or an honor student. If they believe it, they apologize for who they are, try to justify their existence, and expend great energy trying to be something they're not. It is supreme irony that truth-focused people can end up believing and living a lie. When something false seems true to them, they can pass on the possibilities that life has to offer in exchange for living in the hell of their own judgment.

A question I like to ask a Justice is, "On a scale of one to ten with ten being hardest, how hard are you on yourself when you make a mistake?" It is amazing to me how tough Justices can be on themselves. They can deny themselves permission to be human.

At a seminar, I talked to a woman who was 72 years old. She desperately wanted a turning point in her life, but she was terrified that her husband, son and daughter would judge her for selfishly pursuing her own desires. I explained to her the concept of living in the hell of her own judgment. In Disneyland's Haunted House, the ghosts are expressionless, blank statues onto which holograms are projected. Likewise, Justices can project their judgment of themselves onto the blank expressions of those around them. Self-paralysis by judgment is a hellish experience for those who allow this bully into their lives.

If you have an Integrity attribute, you need to ask yourself, "Where are grace, mercy and forgiveness for me as I move forward, making mid-course corrections as needed?" As you inventory the movement and growth in your life, remember to make sure it matches you and not someone with an agenda that doesn't honor the truth about you. Justices have to have an environment where they can grant themselves permission to be human.

I suggest to people with an Integrity attribute that we play a game to see if they can identify themselves. Individuals are designed to respond to guilt in one of three ways; choose which applies to you:

❑ Some people assign the blame to others.
❑ Some people admit what's appropriate and pass on the rest.
❑ Some people take all the guilt on themselves.

Those with an Integrity attribute always pick the third choice. They always identify with total acceptance of guilt. The buck stops with them.

Justices can be counted on for the bottom-line truth, perspective or defined opinion. They help ground others in truth. They help others and themselves move toward integrity in their relationships.

What people physically do with their time and assets is a source of universal guilt. All people think they should be able to do it all and be paragons. This is a sensitive subject and an area that requires permission to be human. Learn to forgive yourself.

CHAPTER 6
PIONEER
from the Growth Family

"A man with enterprise accomplishes more than others because he goes ahead and does it before he is ready."

—Anonymous

Who were those trailblazers, making their way to the land rush in Oklahoma, heading to the Gold Rush in California or drilling for oil in Texas? What about that coach who brought you to the next level? Or that businessman who took his company to dizzying new heights? Where would the space program be without John F. Kennedy's insistence that there be one? They were dynamic people who made a powerful impact on our society.

Pioneers gift people with irresistible hope. They put a fire in our belly. They compel us to move forward, to take the first step and the next step. Recently, my brother Brian, who is a Pioneer, decided we would all do a marathon despite my vigorous objections. He had an answer for every question and a way around every roadblock. Eighteen weeks of training and nine blisters later, I found myself stepping over a finish line I didn't think I could cross.

Pioneers can take us to places we never could have imagined. What price would you pay for the realization of a goal or dream? How valuable would it be to have someone pave the way and show you where to go? Someone to take the bruises for you and to show you where not to venture? Pioneers are easy to spot. They're the ones who are always on the go, looking for growth and movement and overcoming the obstacles. Pioneers won't let you settle for status quo. They're the people who don't accept excuses.

Members of the Growth family have a keen interest in personal success, growth and prestige, and in the development of people, projects, products or businesses. They're aware of growth, and also aware of atrophy and loss in their lives. Pioneers can be described in one word – **momentum**.

They have to progress, to move forward to the next level, the next achievement, the next goal. They are momentum machines, tenacious and determined, with an insatiable appetite for growth. Pioneers must keep moving and growing to be inside their significance. I call it the bulldozer attribute or the pile driver. Sometimes they bulldoze right over their own needs or the needs of their loved ones in order to accomplish what they set out to do.

They are keenly aware of pragmatic, empirical growth and want it to be substantial. So they can be angered by the lack of growth or progress. It can be hard for them to verbalize their dissatisfaction. Instead, they may experience it as a kind of quiet gnawing. These people can walk into a factory and be instantly aware of the volume on the conveyor belt or the lack of it.

As I mentioned previously, there is no hierarchy of abilities. Pioneer is an attribute that throbs...when happy or when oppressed and frustrated. It's one of the first attributes to show up when we do a profile because it involves a level of boundless energy as well as impatience. Pioneers tend to lash out if slowed or stopped. Had they been born in the 19th Century, they'd be participating in the Oklahoma Land Rush; and the moment they planted their flag in the ground, they'd be off to California to pan for gold. After they found their nuggets, they'd rush to Texas to drill for oil. They're designed for movement. Their significance stems from achievement of a goal and then moving to something new. They're either leveraging their achievement, building from it, or simply changing direction.

It is a provocative attribute because it can spur others to move, grow, and transform. It can be relentless and intimidating, but it can also champion others. For their own peace of mind, Pioneers are compelled to track and inventory their movement and growth. Otherwise, they won't have a substantive measure of how much they've grown, how far they've moved, where they've come from, where they've yet to go. At the beginning of every year, a Pioneer I know goes away for a couple of days with his wife to take stock of what they've achieved and to set their new goals. They inventory where they've come from and where they want to go. This measurement gives them a sense of grounding, anchoring, stabilization, competence, and confidence. It's their compass to point them to their true north. The desire for growth needs definitive movement. A dream is a goal without legs. Without movement, it's just a wish...frustrated and frustrating.

Like the markers along the way in a marathon, substantive and experiential milestones are important to Pioneers as a way to know they're moving forward. They must see the signs and experience the experience to validate, nurture, re-energize, and persevere in running toward the finish line. Milestones, goals, something to shoot for and spring-board from are vital and literally directional in nature for them. They need that compass. Without it, they are magnificent ships without direction, sailing around, floundering, looking for a purpose and a port.

Examples of experiential milestones show up in Pioneers' conversations: "We now have the time to take a family vacation" or "I made $10,000 in commissions" or "We just finished renovating the house" or "I saw 25 more clients this year than I did last year" or "I saw 25 fewer clients this year than I did last year."

Pioneers are just as aware of any atrophy in their lives as they are of growth. They have to champion themselves by marking when they grow and move forward.

Pioneers need multiple sources of significance in their

lives. Ronan Tynan, one of The Irish Tenors, exemplifies the unstoppable spirit of the Pioneer. He was a championship equestrian show-jumper. Born with ankle deformity both his lower legs were amputated at age 20. He went on to compete in the Disabled Olympics where he won five Gold medals. Later, he became a doctor. While he was in his medical residency, he entered a singing competition as a tenor where he again won and had the opportunity of touring as professional singer. Ronan Tynan has come full circle to doing singing, touring and breeding horses. Pioneers are happiest when moving to the next level. They don't rest on their laurels. They bulldoze through whatever obstacles they encounter. What fulfills Pioneers is movement.

CHAPTER 7
ARTIST
from the Abstract Family

"Without art, the crudeness of reality would make the world unbearable."

—George Bernard Shaw

What do Martha Stewart and Albert Einstein have in common? They both have the ability to take an abstract thought or concept and turn it into reality. Martha Stewart is an entrepreneur of creative expression. Her fundamental gift is leveraging and building on creative ideas by demonstrating how to bring them into reality via her television program, magazine, products, and books. Albert Einstein used his incredible imagination to seek an understanding of the relationship between time, mass and energy and quantified it in the famous formula $E = mc^2$. His Theory of Relativity revolutionized the laws of physics. He imagined an abstract concept and formulated it to develop the basic building block of nuclear energy.

We might still be in the Dark Ages without artists, inventors, architects and writers. Where would we be without them to distill the worlds of natural and created beauty and catch the subtleties of life; to illuminate the marvels of thought with inventions, graphic art and the written word? They are the inspired, brilliant ones who reinvent the world. Ironically, the abilities that focus on the invisible have the most dramatic and enduring impact on our world. Turn on a light; ride an elevator; hum a tune; read a life-changing book...and you realize the effect of the abstract abilities.

One of my longest friendships is with Annie. She has the gift of celebrating and capturing beauty. My world would have far less color without her. She peels away the layers of reality for me and illuminates the joys, complexities and subtleties of life. She is always interesting and fun. Annie loves to hunt for antiques. Her two homes cannot contain all her romantic treasures, so she has made her hobby work for her by reselling her antiques through Internet auctions! Artistic abilities can be a lifeline, especially when life is heavy with reality. Annie rescued me when I was mired in writing this chapter. She'd been rummaging in an old bookstore and found a tiny book on the joys of writing. At the time, writing was decidedly not joyful for me! By giving me the little book, she helped me break through my writer's block.

It's difficult to define the Artist. How much does your soul weigh? This is by far the family whose characteristic is hardest to nail down. Its undefinability helps to define it. All Abstract abilities are sensitive to environment, and this sensitivity can be to relational, experiential or physical aspects. Because Artists have this sensitivity, they assume others see what they see and feel what they feel. They can become frustrated when others do not appreciate their expressions of this characteristic. Their frustration gives rise to the term "tortured artist". An excellent example of this is Michelangelo, whose frustrations in painting the Sistine Chapel are documented in *The Agony and the Ecstasy*. Where the Justice was intense and dramatic, the Artist from the Abstract family is introspective, subtle and profound. It is extremely important for anyone with this attribute to have an outlet for it. Remember, abilities do not die; they wither and create a throbbing hunger. The key for the Artist is to create something, a physical manifestation of the attribute. It can be a book, a work of art, a structure or an atmosphere; the form is secondary to the need. Creating a physical acknowledgement is essential to achieve a sense of completeness. Without a vehicle for substantively expressing this attribute, the Artist can suffer a bout of abstract constipation.

This attribute is not often discussed in common culture because of its subtlety. Evidence of it is everywhere, but in unsubstantial forms. You can't weigh or inventory the breeze caressing your face, but you must acknowledge its existence.

When unrealized, the Abstract attribute provokes a quiet, soulful frustration, a form of loneliness. The unrealized creative potential of an individual with this attribute can be particularly toxic. When realized, however, the concept, the idea, the creativity being brought into reality brings tremendous personal reward. Unless this ability is actively used on the job, creative pursuits outside the job will be necessary. It is vital for Artists to reward themselves when they meet a deadline, finish a project, or start on a new one. That may mean taking an art class or writing a poem. Engaging this ability prevents the atrophy that comes with disuse.

Artists need to reward themselves to nurture themselves. They don't do well with harsh realities. They find the routine activities of their job dull and boring. For example, the paper-pushing aspects of their daily jobs can be highly toxic for them.

Artists have to find their platform while moving forward in other areas of their lives. Otherwise, they may use their Abstract ability to weave a tapestry of inconsequential imaginings. There are philosophers who won't move forward in their lives because they read their ancient dissertations over and over again for the sheer joy of it. By not leveraging their other abilities, they create toxic environments for themselves and those around them.

Getting out into nature is highly stimulating for those with an Abstract ability. Fellowshipping with nature is important to them because they experience the rush of creation, perfection and symmetry. They are speaking the language of the gods.

This is the attribute most likely to succeed in mirroring back their creation to the Creator. This ability can fast-track into the soul. We need to celebrate them more. People with this attribute are valuable in our lives because they help us all to appreciate the beauty in everything, they make our world more enchanting.

CHAPTER 8
OLYMPIAN
from the Intense Competitor Family

"The greater the difficulty, the more glory in surmounting it."

—Epicurus

Of all the abilities I don't possess, this is the one I wish I had. It's the glorious ability to tenaciously take on challenges, overcome formidable obstacles and emerge victorious. You're fortunate to have an Olympian in your life to help you negotiate a deal, keep a difficult project going, or serve as your advocate. It's great to have someone in your corner, fighting on your behalf.

I met Jeanie years ago. She was in the back of the room at a Seattle seminar with her leg in a cast, propped up on a chair. A single mother of three, barely making it, with no support from her ex-husband, she'd been in an accident that left her with a crushed sternum, broken leg and broken finances. After the seminar, she refocused her energies and fought back, using her Olympian ability with impressive tenacity and determination. She was able to stabilize her finances and her family. Her kids are thriving, and she is now successful. In fact, she has everything she needs to realize her dream: taking on the breath-taking challenge to sell her successful practice and relocate to Maui. Jeanie's Olympian tenacity made it all possible. By her accomplishments, she has inspired her family and many others.

Members of the Intense Competitor family have an intense desire to prevail in life, whether it means winning at all costs or overcoming the obstacles that life presents. Olympians feed off multiple challenges. They realize their significance and gain momentum when they are engaged and stimulated by a variety of personal and professional challenges. If they have only one plate spinning, they tend to procrastinate. They're at their best when attacked, tickled, or intrigued by many things at the same time. Moving to meet those simultaneous challenges is their reward. They're stimulated by having half a dozen plates spinning at the same time. You might say that the diversity of movement moves them. Even in play, they must have the adrenaline surge associated with competitive drive, whether competing with themselves, with others, or with their history.

These multiple challenges need to be homogeneous. What happens to the plate-spinner who has six plates in the air, juggles bowling balls with the feet, and does calligraphy with a pen in the mouth...all at the same time? These are all challenges, but not homogeneous. It's virtually impossible to keep them up. The different demands cause a breakdown of concentration and coordination. When Olympians have too many challenges or dissimilar challenges, it causes breakdown. They are designed to handle half-a-dozen plates.

I tell Olympians that, because they need multiple challenges, they can get over-opportunized very quickly. They may extend themselves until they're a mile wide and an inch deep. Significance comes only from thoughtful pursuit, not from reactive, knee-jerk response. The filter question Olympians have to ask themselves is, "Do I have the time, resources and energy to take on this additional challenge?"

If you are an Olympian, consider this: Take a pen and draw a circle. Make that circle a pie. Cut the pie into slices of significance in your life. Your relationship with your spouse is a slice; your relationship with your children, your work, your philanthropic interest or hobbies are each slices. Let's say your job represents 40 percent of your significance, and the other 60 percent comes from various other areas of your life. Now say you had a bad month in business. That's a minus and draining, but because you've gained significance from other areas of your life, the positives help you through the down times. And they help you when you are not overcoming a challenge.

There is an inherent pride within this ability. It says, "I can do it. I'll be tenacious. I'll be determined. I won't take No for an answer. I'll push myself. I'll push others." Conversely, there is also a smugness saying, "I can't be told No. I won't be told No. I will take on another challenge without removing anything else." As a result, people with this ability become overwhelmed; their resources are diluted, and a mechanism for failure is set up.

Boredom is another mechanism for failure. It occurs when the Competitive attribute is not engaged in the fun of competing. Olympians become bored easily, so they need boredom busters in their world. Golf is a great game for them because they're always competing against themselves and they'll never master the game. It's like a chew toy for a pet. It allows the Olympian attribute to engage and to gnaw at something without gnawing at themselves, their world or their relationships. Through golf, they are able to use their tenacious ability in an appropriate manner. The attribute always needs to be engaged: it's just a matter of how you choose to engage it.

This characteristic can be dangerous to their own growth and success because Olympians love to start things over from scratch. People with this attribute tend to continually re-invent themselves, their environment and relationships. They keep hitting their heads on the midway point of success and significance, fully aware that there is a higher level, and they start all over again. In effect, they unwittingly sabotage themselves so as not to be bored. They love the adrenaline surge of starting over. But they cannot have a stabilized, balanced environment with success and significance if they themselves constantly ruin or revamp their world. The constant changes of direction and the over-opportunization cause burnout.

Some Olympians sell very different types of products, all at the same time, because it is easy for them to start new endeavors from scratch. Or they may pursue multiple career paths. By doing this, they're not really creating the vocation or lifestyle they're looking for. In a way, they are demonstrating perseverance through tenacity and determination. Well, that's wonderful, but it's not good for them. They are only evidencing their reactive muscle memory when they keep starting over from scratch. "Let me change careers. Let me go in a new direction. Let me try this and that." The older they get, the more frustrated they become with themselves. They know there's more they could be doing and more available resources they're not using when they keep starting over. Some only get to Level 5 in their lives instead of Level 10.

Olympians are obsessive, and they strive to reach the highest level. If an area of their lives is not going well, they need to put it in maintenance mode and transfer their focus to another area. A positive example of this attribute is Muhammad Ali. He has overcome the greatest challenges of life, professional and personal, including Parkinson's disease, to be an exemplary goodwill ambassador around the world.

CHAPTER 9
PERFORMER
from the Impress Family

"There is nothing harder than the softness of indifference."

—Juan Montalvo

As an Olympian loves challenges, the Performer is challenged by provoking a response from an audience. Both pursue their goals with the same tenacity. Performers are the provocateurs who swim against the current and start new trends. Without them, we'd all live in the same boxes.

How dull our lives would be without entertainers and high-performance athletes! What would be our inspiration if we had no one to amaze us or make us laugh or entertain us? How boring would school have been without the class cut-up? Performers delight in making others think, feel and respond positively to living outside the box. Remember the first grade teacher who left an indelible stamp on your spirit? Or the friend who prompted you to move in a new direction you'd never have thought of yourself? The Depression would have been harder to bear without Chaplin, Keaton, Laurel and Hardy. Wars would have been total hell without Bob Hope and the USO. Young people would miss the niceties of political satire without Saturday Night Live and Late Show monologues. The antics of Robin Williams and Jim Carey delight us. The showmanship of the Harlem Globetrotters entertains and amazes us. Performers light up the world. They energize a room. They provoke others to feel, think, laugh, get out of the mundane or mediocre. So what if they're showing off? That's their thing! Performers have to wow us with excellence. Everything is a performance, including how they enter a room. They love to be at center-stage.

The worst thing for them is trying to win over an audience that won't react. Performers are allergic to unresponsiveness. They break out in hives when they encounter it. Because they're highly sensitive to the nature of response, indifference is their Achilles heel. For an Impress person to feel satisfied, the audience must register enthusiasm. Performers need to remind themselves that others may not naturally be responsive. If ignored, Performers feel like part of the wallpaper and may act out inappropriately. This is their greatest disability. They'll go around provoking others in any way they can, living life in a drama department of their own making. When unmanaged, this can become quite negative, intentionally to provoke a response.

Our society doesn't know what to do with these people, but we need their ability. Our recognition of their value goes back to the time of court jesters. Society has always needed entertainment. Performers are wonderful in their ability to amuse, shock, and provoke us...to make us think and feel differently.

While they love an audience, Impress people are not generally responsive themselves and do not make a good audience. They tend to want to reserve the wow response for themselves. This is often evident at awards shows, especially at the Oscars, where practiced civility and graciousness replace real enthusiasm.

Performers have a natural ability to be noticed and remembered. At the grocery store, strangers come up to them and gush, "Oh my Gosh, how are you? How are the kids? How are things going?" Performers cultivate recognition on a subconscious level. A businessman would need to spend thousands of dollars on marketing materials to be noticed and remembered to the same degree. Impress people are naturally endowed with the greatest marketing tool – presence. That alone represents and sells them. Presence motivates and influences others. It's a marvelous gift and a pragmatic tool.

The Impress ability doesn't require its owner to be dramatic. People with this ability can move quietly through a group of people and still be noticed, acknowledged and welcomed. They use the environment to be noticed. Quiet or dramatic, those with an Impress ability are always aware of their relationships, surroundings and position. They seek to be valued by being acknowledged.

My youngest brother Kevin has three abilities from the Impress family. Things are never dull in his world. He is about impressing others with quick-witted humor and provocative insights. If Kevin is in the mood, he can change the emotional temperature in the entire family from subdued to raucous within five minutes. It requires no effort for him to do this. His presence brightens our lives and restores our mood, humor, and enthusiasm. When he was a teenager, he had a job at a bowling alley as a janitor. Now, this is traditionally an obscure job. But everyone leaks who they are, and Kevin's impress abilities transformed the job "slightly." He'd take large plastic garbage bags, use them as a cape, and run through the bowling alley as Captain Garbage, super-hero of trash collection.

It's not hard to figure out that Kevin was celebrated almost entirely for making others laugh. Fast-forward to an adult problem Kevin experienced. His profession required him to handle hundreds of thousands of dollars for his clients, but he had a problem with people seeing him as a serious professional. His profile shows he has the gift of insight and creative thought. He is able to negotiate and process thoughts quickly. Whenever Kevin came to hear me speak, I always went to him for input afterward. I knew he would immediately have a valid feel for how effective I was with the audience. Any critical insights of his were always perceptive, true and appreciated by me. Until recently, Kevin had never consciously chosen to change how he is perceived by those in his sphere of influence. He now makes a conscious choice to show up inside his business. By that I mean the dialogue he uses professionally now focuses on his abilities of clear insight, thinking outside the box and quick thinking. He is still outrageously funny in his personal life, but he puts forth a casual, amiable, yet professional style in his business. It has created phenomenal results for him and has boosted his competence and confidence. If there is someone in your life that you delight in talking to or who puts a smile on your face, most likely they have an Impress ability.

Like Justices, Performers can be particularly sensitive to the nurture they received. They may have had stoic parents and been punished for acting dramatically. Perhaps they were told that they should be seen but not heard. The Performer can be funny and dramatic, but also extremely toxic.

There are three basic ways to show internal integrity:

❏ by following traditional right/wrong, black/white ethics and values;

❏ by manifesting excellence

❏ by impacting an individual, organization or audience.

Performers demonstrate their integrity through impact. They're designed to have an effect on you.

Those with the Impress ability can make good salespeople. But boy, can they be sold a bill of goods themselves! They'll have a garage full of Ab-rollers, Thighmasters, Nordic Traks, and all the latest computer gadgets. They can be sold anything and end up with buyer's remorse. They enjoy the give-and-take of selling and buying. They like the repartee and response.

In general, people with the Impress ability are hypersensitive to how they're perceived. What happens if they make a mistake? What if they fall on their face? What happens if they fail to impress?! It creates a defensiveness in them.

One of my staff became confident and comfortable with the Ability Management process only when she was able to set aside her Impress attribute. She did this by telling herself, "I'm owning this information irrespective of how I'm perceived and regardless of how I'm being responded to." That set her free to embrace the process and enthusiastically do her job. Up to that point, she had been somewhat tentative in her manner, not because she did not believe in the value of what she did, but for fear of how the person at the other end might perceive her.

Sometimes it's necessary to say really hard things to people. Those with an Impress attribute can do this with humor so the message can be received without hard feelings.

Direct predators for an Impress person are people with Structure attributes. Ask Impress realtors, "Have you ever worked for an analytical, cerebral, engineer-type client?" If they have, they will tell you that it drove them crazy, because they didn't know where they stood with their client. There was no laughter, wow, verbal acknowledgment or applause to indicate how well the realtor® was doing. Analytical, cerebral, intellectual, facilitative people are naturally frustrating for the Impress person.

Performers regard others as mirrors back to them. Responses are milestones. But, there is a temporary nature to their impress. Response is like a rich, cream-filled dessert that is left unrefrigerated. It's beautiful and sumptuous today, but turns bad tomorrow. You're only as good as your last role.

That's the pressure in Hollywood that results in substance abuse. Actors and musicians are raised to stardom and then quickly fall from favor. Gwyneth Paltrow may've been the toast of the town a month ago, but this week she's considered bland. Dennis Rodman did increasingly outlandish things to get a response. Some Performers finally get the response they've wanted and find themselves trapped in a specific role. They can only perform a certain way or remain in the same sitcom. Some want a response so badly that they get trapped in a vicious cycle, doing more and more to shock or provoke, leading to a tabloid ending.

CHAPTER 10
ENGINEER
from the Structure Family

"To have his path made clear for him is the aspiration of every human being in our beclouded and tempestuous existence."

—Joseph Conrad

Our civilization is built on layers of structure, operating procedures and quality control. Would you be comfortable driving across a bridge built without plans? Do you know someone who loves to organize an office, garage or kitchen, helping to create a sense of order? How many movers and shakers would be dynamically effective without the people who hold it all together behind the scenes? Engineers are as invaluable to society as they are invisible.

People with Structure family attributes think in terms of structure: charts, pictures, graphs, compartments. They are focused on how to...with pragmatism and a processing bent. They say things like, "Just tell me how!" and "Don't motivate me or BS me. Tell me how to do it."

Those with a low tolerance for handling logistics and structure would be jello without the mold if they couldn't rely on

Structure people for order. Engineers don't toot their own horns, and they work mostly behind the scenes. That is where they quietly find their significance, as foundational influences in society.

I'm like the nutty professor, bouncing around from thought to action to thought. I'm told that talking to me is like sipping water from a fire hydrant. Imagine my difficulty in writing a linear, logical book in orderly, sequential chapters. One of my editors has the Engineer ability. He makes order out of chaos, and I follow his direction.

I know an attorney who was an only child with minimal parental involvement in his childhood. He lived most of his adult life alone and married late in life. He and his wife adopted a two-month-old boy from an Eastern-bloc country. This attorney had a fiery temper and virtually no experience at nurturing relationships. Initially, I was nervous about him being thrown into instant parenthood. Later, I was gladdened by his startling transformation into fatherhood. He used his Structural ability to clarify what the role of father required of him. He concentrated on the process needed to make him supportive, nurturing, gentle and patient. With a serious focus, he implemented the required steps. Now it's second nature to him. He experiences the joys of successful parenting and continues to amaze me.

Engineers have tremendous assurance. They can build the Golden Gate Bridge; no problem. They're forceful and implement doggedly. However, they won't move forward without a blueprint. They need structure before execution. Goals, aspirations and expectations must be specific. Structure is how they process and progress. You can be sure that they will build the plans according to the specifications. Structure is an essential component for their greenhouse to grow their competence and confidence. Their instructions must be linear and logical with step-by-step details. This ability becomes passive without a blueprint. Too abstract or conceptual, and they're lost. You can't tell Engineers to just bake a cake; you have to give them the recipe. (The book *Who Moved My Cheese?* by Spencer Johnson is excellent for those with Structure abilities.)

Engineers act mainly on what they process. They can be resistant to change, analytical, stoic, and critical of themselves. Instead, they ought to celebrate being analytical. That's how they function!

An advantage of this ability is that they hold things together. They maintain things. They can achieve the needed results, but also can conflict with entrepreneurial abilities. Those who have this attribute can be bureaucratic when it comes to painting outside the lines. The Structure ability can be prized in some environments and dismissed, resented or opposed in others. Engineers can frustrate colleagues with their strong adherence to the way things have always been. Engineers must remember that saying No to change cuts them off from creativity and growth. They can be so structured that it inhibits growth or change. They can cast themselves so strongly in a specific mold that they have to be jackhammered out of it. Transition is a roller coaster ride for Engineers. By being specific and literal and giving them progressive steps to follow, those who work with Engineers can make any anticipated transitions easier for them.

Again, if you have this ability, don't assume that everyone else has it.

CHAPTER 11
REFINER
from the Discern Family

"Keep away from people who try to belittle your ambitions. Small people always do that, but the really great make you feel that you, too, can become great."

—Mark Twain

Designer, counselor, stylist, surgeon, coach, editor. Refiners will not let us settle for mediocrity. They insist that we go for the gold and give our best. Our lives would be far less without their insights, discernment and passion to make the world the best it can be. Can you picture yourself driving a Model T to work or going to the doctor for your weekly leeching? What about wearing the latest in sackcloth or homespun fashion from the runways of Milan and Paris? Refiners help us progress. They love to enrich and improve people, places and things. They inspire others to improve themselves, to reach beyond what they know and think possible.

As a Refiner, I am delighted that my improved profiling methodology has been enthusiastically and popularly received.

I combined old-world concepts, observational analysis, natural empathy and word pictures and refined them to make profiles more easily and better understood. My goal was to create a simplified language that everyone could use without having a Ph.D. When people ask me how I did it, I tell them I just saw it. I saw the possibilities by looking beyond what there was to what there could be. My brother Brian is also a Refiner. He took the simple concept of word-of-mouth referrals and developed it into a powerful tool for relational marketing referral businesses. He now heads the largest, most successful coaching company in America, and he is still refining, enriching and improving.

Members of the Discern family have an above-average grasp of unseen factors in a given situation. They use their unique capability of seeing what's ahead down the road to clarify big-picture jobs and projects and improve them. Unlike the Performer's ability to be seen, this is the ability to see. Simply put, those with Discern attributes have an x-ray eye.

This is a truth-teller ability. For Refiners, the truth they see can get them into trouble and cause them heartache. I liken them to messengers in ancient times. What did they do to the messenger if they didn't like the message? They killed the messenger. Refiners can be vilified for their insights and discernment. I tell them, "You can see train wrecks before they happen. For you, it's logical and natural to look ahead. Others may not share this ability. Their short-sightedness and disbelief may contribute to the wreck." I advise those with a Discern ability to use it first on themselves by asking, "Is this the highest and best use of my time? Is this an audience capable of hearing what I have to say? Can they bear the truth?" By asking questions of their audience to feel them out, they are in a better position to decide whether it would be helpful or hurtful to share what they see.

Refiners are designed to see what's wrong with the world. However, they must be invited to contribute or share this information. Without request or invitation, if Refiners present visions that are troubling or negative they may be perceived by their audience as judgmental, overly critical, or tyrannical. Refiners don't see it that way. They only want to make things better. Refiners can also have a pragmatic motivation and want to see substantial change.

The Refiner ability makes for a wonderful parent. Those who have this attribute want to encourage their children to be the best they can be. But this same ability can turn a nurturing mother or father into a tyrant. So, son Johnny can run for all he's worth and do the hundred yards in 15.2 seconds and hear from the Refiner parent: "Son, that was great, but if you tried harder, you could do it in 14.8 seconds." Or, daughter Amy might come home with a B+ and hear, "Well, Amy, if you studied harder and watched less TV, you could get an A." Refiners have to be careful not to overdo it.

Inefficiency makes Refiners irritable. I'll use myself as an example. When my wife grabs the wrong side of the sheet when we make the bed...because she's left-handed...I get annoyed. Actually, I'm annoyed by the inefficiency. Refiners are control-oriented. They can end up organizing their sock drawer as a way of controlling their environment.

Anyone with a Discern attribute is immediately aware of not growing and moving toward what they're designed to do. It's tough on them to feel they're out of control. They may grip the steering wheel so tightly that they lose control of the car. They tend to hyper-focus on the wrong control issues...minor inefficiencies or displeasure at their own imagined lack of organization.

Because Refiners are designed to improve or enhance, they can be opinionated. They have a sincere desire to make things better and a tremendous ability to see beyond a problem to refinements and solutions. However, they tread on others' toes when they try to fix things that are not theirs to fix. Occasionally, their perception is off, but they see it as correct. It's not about opinions; it's about what they see and how they see it. Sometimes they don't have all the information they need.

In *The 7 Habits of Highly Effective People*, Stephen R. Covey tells a story about himself riding the subway. A father with two small sons got on and sat next to Covey. The children ran up and down the car, raising cain and bumping into passengers. Covey discerned that the father was a poor parent because he didn't seem to have the ability to stop his sons from misbehaving. He shared this insight with the father, who replied, "We have come from the hospital where their mother just died. What do I tell them?"

Refiners mine diamonds in the sense that they actively

seek the best and look for perfection. The passive side of this ability can unwittingly make them enablers. Discerners may see another person for what that person can become and fail to consider all the factors. They see unrealized potential and try to draw it out, but the person may have no desire to cooperate. Discerners can create a passive, enabling environment and set the person up to disappoint them. That person will never realize the potential the Discerner saw. Discerners must learn to look for green lights before they move forward.

A story to illustrate these points. A woman with a Discern attribute falls in love with Oscar Madison. One day, she sees him pick up a piece of paper, and she is so happy! She says to herself, "Hey, if I just put a trash can here and a laundry basket there, and we have a housekeeper two days a week, this relationship can work! I can improve that slob, Oscar, into the neat, wonderful Felix Unger that I want. Well, they get married, and Oscar moves in. She finds out that her new hubby loves being a slob. He's not Felix. He loves being Oscar! She's married to chaos, and that can be supremely frustrating.

Oprah had a guest who said, "When someone shows you who they are, believe them." That is terrific advice for those with a Discern ability.

Because Refiners have this ability, they assume other people have it. And, they're indignant when others don't act on it, as they do. Say that someone runs into a brick wall. If you have a Discern attribute, you can see from far off that it's not a door. Your first reaction is: What kind of idiot is that? or: Why didn't they see that?

Those with a Discern attribute have less tolerance or empathy when people make mistakes repeatedly.

CHAPTER 12
SCHOLAR
from the Learn Family

"Every age has its own outlook. It is specially good at seeing certain truths and specially liable to make certain mistakes. We all, therefore, need the books that will correct the characteristic mistakes of our own period. And that means the old books."

—C.S. Lewis

Scholars are compelled to discover and acquire knowledge. Teacher, scientist, explorer, historian, anthropologist, theologian...all are examples of scholars. Those with the gift of learning open new worlds for us. These perpetual students remind us who we are and how we relate to our world. They help us celebrate the fascination of life.

They love to be immersed in the school of life, books, tapes, classes and people. This quest is their fountain of youth. As long as they keep learning, they feel alive. They regard learning as a never-ending journey, and the process of learning and understanding is exciting to them. Scholars love to learn, not only the things they have to learn, but any and all things. As perpetual students, they constantly find new intellectual challenges.

To ever-hungry Scholars, knowledge is like a cruise ship buffet. There are so many wonderful dishes to try! They read about anything and everything, and they can discuss myriad subjects with anyone they meet. And they find everyone interesting because they learn from them. Scholars can digest huge amounts of information and can actually learn for others. They are knowledge boosters...walking, talking resources for other people...human encyclopedias.

One of the coaches we worked with, Jody, had a voracious appetite for learning. She became the reference librarian for the coaching department because she gathered a vast amount of coaching knowledge and information and shared it with the other coaches. She made them better by her own desire to learn. As is the way with Scholars, she was compelled to move on to new areas of intellectual and artistic stimulation. She learned and owned her profile, and mustered the courage to move through many roadblocks in her life to pursue next-level growth.

The effectiveness of Scholars can be diluted when they try to learn too much at once because everything interests and intrigues them. They get caught up in academic pursuits and forget about the practical aspects of their subject. This can be frustrating to colleagues, friends and families. They are over-using their minds at the expense of other areas of their lives.

They have to ask, "What can I do with my knowledge to move my business forward? How will this new knowledge improve my life?" These practical applications will help them focus on moving forward in their lives. Scholars must also make sure they constantly learn about their chosen profession. This will prevent the frustration and boredom that goes with repetitive tasks.

There are other questions Scholars need to ask themselves on a daily basis to remain stimulated and vital: "What did I learn today? What can I learn today about being a better manager and better motivator?" For Scholars, no learning equals no vitality. They need to work in environments that encourage their appetite for interesting, diverse learning.

Anyone with a Learn ability inherently assumes that everyone learns. From my coaching experience, I've noted that Learn people become frustrated with the slowness to learn of others. Those with Learn abilities learn from their mistakes readily and efficiently. Because it's natural for them, they don't realize that others may not naturally learn as readily or efficiently.

The Learn attribute can show up in a variety of ways: love of discovery, travel, and new experiences; love of solving mysteries, puzzles or problems; and as the desire to learn that which can be of practical use.

CHAPTER 13
FREE SPIRIT
from the Intense Freedom Family

"To know how to free oneself is nothing; the arduous thing is to know what to do with one's freedom."

—Andre Gide

The rebel, negotiator, radical, adventurer, free-thinker. In our institutions, who watches out for the gullible? Who shows you the art of play? Who helps you to paint outside the lines? Where would we be without those who have a healthy distrust of the System, protecting us from Big Brother? Throughout history Free Spirits have made up the underground resistance movements, standing up against institutional tyranny.

I am naturally gullible because I give people the benefit of the doubt and rarely does it occur to me to have any doubt. If I didn't have Free Spirits in my life I'd own a lot of London bridges. I'm grateful to have a Free Spirited attorney; he can easily paint another perspective for me. He can read between the lines to illuminate a hidden agenda. That provides me with great peace of mind. I don't see what he sees. I need his contrary position to protect me from my blind spots.

Free Spirits can be fun and stimulating. They can also have the attitude, "Don't tick me off. Don't nag me!" Free Spirits can instantaneously feel encroached upon. They can be viewed as rebels, undisciplined, contrary, anti-social, inflexible, lazy, or irresponsible. This is one of the most intense and misunderstood abilities. Our common culture sees Free Spirits as either the "easy rider" image or as lazy. But there is much more richness to a Free Spirit than that.

The richness of Free Spirits is in how they can paint outside the lines, that is, they can think outside the box. Tremendous cultural strides have been made because a Free Spirit asked, "Does it really have to be done that way? Does it have to flow this way? Do we have to adhere to this rule?" The strength of a Free Spirit is ingenuity. Because they are always questioning, always looking for angles, they can come up with some very creative ideas and solutions to problems.

Free Spirits are self-motivated and independent. They can swim upstream. You absolutely can't "guilt" a Free Spirit. They are not sensitive to the hissing snake.

Free Spirits are compelled to be free. I always ask my Free Spirit clients, "What does a wolf do when it gets its leg caught in a bear trap?" And they always know the answer: "It chews its own leg off to escape." That's exactly what a Free Spirit does. They cannot stand to be in bondage; they have to be independent; they have to be free.

The thing with their freedom is that it's personal, independent freedom. The moment you interject another relationship, there's another natural agenda that can seem to bring bondage. Free Spirits are claustrophobic. They need to be given lots of room. You have to let them fly away to come back to you. Like a falcon to a glove, you have to let them go to come back. It's beyond the horizon of someone who's not a Free Spirit to see how far they have to go to come back. But they will come back if they feel they can trust you.

Although Free Spirits resist and dislike bondage, when this ability is not properly managed, they end up in some form of environmental or relational bondage. The poster child for misusing this attribute is Dennis Rodman. Frequently, debt is the wolf trap for them. They give their freedom over to it.

They need to learn to work smart so they can have more freedom. When communicating with Free Spirits, use the "F"-word...FREEDOM: "How can I free you up?" "I want to set you free to do more interesting things." "If you can find time to work on this, I can free you up to move on to better things." You cannot approach a Free Spirit with "You should do this..." but rather, "Would you prefer choice A or choice B?" Choices are important to Free Spirits. They want fences that keep others out, but not fences that keep them in. They resist structure because they view it as oppression. In reality they need to reach out to others to help co-create structure for them. Once structure is established they are then truly free to play. Free Spirits are designed to play their way to success and significance. The more freedom they have the happier they are.

To prevent burnout in their jobs or relationships, it is critical that they honor their free-spirited nature in their private lives. They must get out into nature and do things they want to do. They must exercise their Free Spirit on a regular basis. This will give them the proper balance between success and freedom, and others will be drawn to that balance.

An example of someone who manages his Free Spirit well from a professional standpoint would be Ted Turner. He's independent, free. He owns the largest ranch in Montana. He is reported to have walked into his board of directors and said, "I want a global satellite news network. I'm going sailing and when I get back I want you to tell me how we're going to do it."

CHAPTER 14
HOW YOU USE YOUR ABILITIES
Work Styles

"A musician must make music, an artist must paint, a poet must write, if he is to be at peace with himself. What a man can be, he must be. "

—Abraham Maslow

My purpose is to provide practical wisdom you can immediately start applying to your life. Everyone has five or six dominant abilities. From the ten families of abilities we've reviewed, list only those abilities that strongly resonate with you. As mentioned earlier, how you use your natural abilities is as important as the abilities you've been given. Based on their styles and perspectives, two people with the same five or six dominant abilities can look quite dissimilar in how they work, parent, and relate to others. Each needs a different environment to grow, learn and thrive. One of them may value tangible results while the other values experiences and feelings. One may enjoy the company of others nearly all the time, whereas the other might need regular time alone to reflect and rejuvenate. One may work slowly and meticulously while the other moves fast to get a lot accomplished in a short time. One might live in the present moment while the other lives with a view of the future in mind.

No matter what your work style, enjoying your profession and knowing how to relate well to others are important to success. In *The Millionaire Mind*, Dr. Thomas J. Stanley reports the results of his survey of five thousand millionaires. One thousand responded with full disclosure. The researchers then interviewed 775 of the responding millionaires in depth. Across the board, all the millionaires stated that they enjoyed their profession and that this enjoyment was a high priority for them. Fifty-eight percent declared it essential to have good personal and professional relationships. Relational sophistication was Extremely Important or Very Important to their career success.

As you discover who you are and find what you enjoy doing, your chances of achieving the success you were made for increase greatly.

There are three distinct work styles: Motivators, Facilitators, and Strategists. Perhaps you can identify something of yourself in each, but you're seeking your dominant style. You may be able to recognize it by its positive effects. However, it will probably be easier to identify your dominant style of work by how it gets you in trouble.

Motivators help us move to the next level in our lives. They gain significance from creating movement in others or helping others shift their point of view. Examples of Motivators are: the teacher who championed you to consider a certain vocation;

the coach who made you believe in yourself; the fitness instructor who encouraged you to lose weight. In isolation, believing in yourself is not easy. We need impetus from others to inspire, encourage and champion our achievements.

Winston Churchill is a superb example of the Motivator on a grand scale. In World War II, he inspired England to persevere despite constant bombings, devastating losses, limited war materials and rationed food. Motivators are verbally dynamic. They can actively create the "ah-ha" experience and influence people to think in a different way. They look for ways to create win-win situations and opportunities to promote a cause, idea, action or sale. Motivators use their knowledge, passion and vision to persuade. Because they're verbally dynamic, they're good negotiators. They are perceived as traditional salespeople or impassioned advocates.

While Motivators possess the natural ability to work hard, they don't naturally work smart. They tend to do things themselves that they'd be smarter to have someone else do. They must learn to work smart...when to delegate tasks and when to seek the expertise of others.

Facilitators are designed to create an environment for change and growth. They naturally monitor, nurture and manage. The listening ear is invaluable. Receptivity and perspective from someone who sees the entire picture are essential. The therapist or doctor, the friend who takes time to listen to you, the parent who gives you room to move and grow at your own pace — they're all Facilitators.

They naturally survey and inventory their surroundings, listening for a dialogue and looking for the green light in any situation or relationship. When the green light goes on in a selling relationship, for example, Facilitators proceed with confidence. In sales, they shine when they invite others to the table and respectfully allow them to make their own decision.

Arguably, the most powerful man in America is Alan Greenspan, Chairman of The Federal Reserve Board. He spends most of his time analyzing and inventorying the economy. He doesn't say much, but when he does, everyone listens.

Because Facilitators don't like to be forced or manipulated, they tend to censor themselves so they will not be considered pushy or offensive. Due to their self-censoring, Facilitators are often considered non-traditional salespeople. They're rewarded when they get others to make decisions with minimal interference on the Facilitator's part.

Facilitators have a natural ability to work hard and work smart. Their disability is a tendency to be passive, waiting for the go-ahead from others.

Strategists make good leaders because they consciously create environments for us to be safe and dynamic, to have clarity and hope. Once Strategists create the right environment, they have a natural ability to infuse that environment with enthusiasm, inspiration and leadership.

Nowadays, they're known as executive types. American literature celebrates a young executive type named Tom Sawyer. When given the task of whitewashing a long fence, he inventoried his environment, provided brushes and paint, then got his friends to see the fun they'd miss if they didn't join in. He got everyone else to do his work enthusiastically.

During World War II, if General MacArthur had been removed from his headquarters, handed a rifle and sent to the front lines, it wouldn't have been the highest and best use of his abilities. It certainly wouldn't have been in the best interests of the U.S. military. MacArthur had an army to implement his strategy. Those with this ability need a supporting staff to be successful. Without a team to carry out what they envision, Strategists become, like a bug on its back, helpless to move forward. That is their disability. Most of the time, Strategists work smart since they have no problem delegating. It's when they can't delegate that they become ineffective.

My brother Brian, a Strategist, was preparing to speak to several hundred people at a retreat in Oregon. He decided to make some changes to the workbooks that the attendees would be using the next day. That required his staff to open hundreds of binders and replace 2,500 pages. A bellman brought all the workbook boxes to Brian's suite. I arrived late to help. As I opened the suite door, a cacophony of sounds greeted me: "I need more blues. I need more reds!"; binders popping open and snapping shut. People were stepping over each other, and crumpled paper was piling up in the corner of the room. Meanwhile, Brian was sitting on the bed, addressing the troops: "And tomorrow morning we're going to do this and then we're going to do that.... When this happens, we will do this!" He was General MacArthur motivating his staff. As I sat down on the edge of the bed, I noticed there were no binders on the bed. I looked at him and said, "You're not going to help, are you?" In response, he rose to his full stature and said with a smile, "That's not who I am. It's not what I do." He went right back to talking to the troops.

Listeners to this story have pointed out to me that I came late, sat on the edge of the bed, and didn't help either! For all the years I've told this story, I've left out that part. Now I need to come clean, neither of us helped. We're both Strategists.

If you are a Strategist, you're not naturally designed to execute physically what you plan mentally. The best use of your natural work style is to inventory your surroundings, create an environment, then motivate within that environment to build synergy, clarity, action stages or positive experiences.

Strategists are adept at leveraging their resources and environments. This includes using emotions, physical assets, financial resources and especially the natural abilities of others. They are clinical in their assessments and wonderfully insightful about who would be good for accomplishing particular tasks. Strategists have a strong leadership characteristic. They evaluate people and situations for potential, leadership and growth. They also look for those who can follow their lead and physically execute their vision. They're trying to figure out how to get the best out of the system. They can be extremely personal, warm and friendly, but they're always using that eagle eye to survey their professional and personal environment to see who can accomplish their vision.

Strategists generally feel helpless when they have to carry out their own plans. Most are all thumbs when it comes to the actual doing. They don't have the patience for it. Because of their natural discernment, they know that execution is not their thing.

How you work doesn't apply just to your job; it applies to everything...parenting, hobbies, volunteering. *Your work style is the filter all your natural abilities go through.* If you have a natural ability to take on challenges, for example, that ability can play out in different ways, depending on your work style. The Motivator says, "I'll take on the challenge myself." The Facilitator ponders, "I wonder when I should take on this challenge?" The Strategist asks, "Who can I get to take on this challenge for me?"

A realtor was showing houses to a couple for more than six months. The realtor, a Facilitator, eventually threw up her hands in frustration because she couldn't get the couple to make a decision. Her partner offered to try. After examining the needs and concerns of the clients, he called the couple. He said, "Based on my research, the house you just saw is the type of house you would be interested in. To best serve you, it would help me to know what you liked and did not like about the house". The couple's fundamental objection was revealed when they replied, "For 1.5 million dollars, we wanted a kitchen with better lighting". They talked about how to solve the lighting problem and made an offer the next day. Assertive communication ended six months of passivity.

In order to sell effectively, you have to know your own natural work style and speak in the natural language of your clients...even though it may not be your own natural language. This applies in any situation where you want to get another person to consider your ideas: talking with your spouse about where you'd like to go on vacation or discussing with your daughter why she should do her chores or meeting with your boss concerning why you believe you deserve a promotion. Awareness of your own natural style and of the other person's style and language can have a tremendous positive effect.

Work style can make a sale or break a sale. Sometimes you see this manifested both ways on the same shopping expedition. A while ago, I bought a luxury car. My friends were giving me a hard time about it because my car was much nicer than my wife's. So my wife Joan, a Facilitator, and I, a Strategist, went to check out local Mercedes dealerships with the idea of evening things up by getting her a better car. We were accompanied by one of our best friends, a Motivator, who is a natural negotiator.

At the first dealership, we spoke to a salesperson who was a Facilitator. He greeted us without leaving his desk. We walked around looking at the cars in his showroom. He didn't actively engage in conversation, but said, "If you have any questions, just ask."

We said, "Thank you." Later, we asked him for information about a particular platinum-colored model, its features, etc. He answered all our questions. Our Motivator friend had come along to help with the negotiations and was disappointed that the Facilitator salesman wouldn't negotiate. The salesman simply said, "I'll take $3,000 off for cash and that's my final offer." He wouldn't engage in any further talk about it. He was polite and answered all our questions, but wouldn't negotiate.

We decided to go to the next dealership. It was much larger and had about ten times the inventory of the first. No sooner had we closed our car door and started walking around the lot than we were greeted by, "Hey, how ya' doin'? What's goin' on? It's a beautiful day, isn't it?" This was a Motivator salesman. He was friendly and dynamic with much knowledge and enthusiasm.

Well, I learned a great deal about Mercedes cars from that gentleman. He had 30 years of automobile sales experience. He was confident in his delivery, expertise and inventory. However, he and Joan had different work styles; She's a Facilitator and he a Motivator. He did most of the talking and never listened to her. When he pointed out a green Mercedes, my wife told him, "Actually, we already have a spruce-green Mercedes. I don't want us to be twins in the garage and get mixed up. I'd really like a different color."

He tried to persuade her by pointing out that they were slightly different color greens. We ended up test-driving the green Mercedes because the Motivator wanted us to drive the green Mercedes. As we walked back to our own car, he continued to be dynamic and forceful, asking, "What can I do to get you to sign on the dotted line?" My wife became quieter and quieter. We excused ourselves to think it over. Joan shot the deal down with one sentence, "He isn't listening to me."

From whom do you think we bought the car? My wife went back to the Facilitator salesman and purchased a car from him. The Motivator salesman lost the sale because he had inadvertently pushed her away. He didn't listen to what she wanted and bulldozed right through her. And while we were signing the contract, the Facilitator salesman bemoaned the fact that he lost many sales because he doesn't negotiate well. How frustrating! Both salesmen lose sales...one because he pushes too hard, the other because he is too passive.

From another perspective, both men suffered loss of sales for the same reasons: because they weren't aware of how they sell and because they didn't realize how their audience needed to be sold. These salespeople did not effectively communicate with their clients.

What is your natural work style?

Here are some quick ways to determine your style.

You are a Facilitator if the following statements fit your philosophy and method of selling:

I am encouraged when...

❏   I provide information to potential buyers so they can make a decision.

❏   I provide a valuable service to buyers.

❏   I show respect for potential buyers.

You are a Motivator if the following statements fit your philosophy and method of selling:

I am encouraged when...

❏ I help shape and influence a potential buyer's perspective.

❏ I positively impact the buyer's decision.

❏ I present a thoughtful, persuasive idea to potential buyers.

You are a Strategist if:

❏ You own the sales agency.

❏ You get Motivators and Facilitators to sell for you.

Positive Request. Ask your client this: "In order for me to serve you better, please tell me about a positive experience you've had with a salesperson. The answer defines the type of salesperson your client DOES WANT.

If you know your natural selling style and the style your client needs, you can adapt your sales presentation accordingly. Give your Facilitator clients a comfortable, respectful environment, including time to think about their decision. Facilitator clients need to know you've heard them. Demonstrate this by stating their needs and wants back to them as you understand them. Check with them to assure you've got it right and to reassure them. Help them overcome any passivity or indecisiveness. You can share your own expertise by suggesting, "If it were me, I would ..." or "If I were in this situation, I'd ... because..."

Your Motivator clients need to know that you are focusing on results and representing them well. Let them know how you

What selling style does your client want? Here are some tips to determine the sales style that will appeal to your client:

POSITIVE REQUEST

Ask your client this: "In order for me to serve you better, please tell me about a positive experience you've had with a salesperson.
The answer defines the type of salesperson your client
DOES WANT.

FACILITATOR	MOTIVATOR
• Made me feel comfortable.	• Created a win-win situation.
• Available to advise me.	• Negotiated with my best interests in mind.
• Did not pressure me to make a decision.	• Presented options I would never have considered
• Was respectful of my needs.	• Showed me the best buy and encouraged me to go for it.

will work for them. Listen to them and be patient.

With self-awareness, everyone can learn to work smart. To begin managing your work style, ask yourself what structure, time, and resources you need for balance. If you're a Facilitator, ask yourself if you need movement to counteract your natural passivity. If you're a Motivator, do you need perspective from someone else to validate your environment? If you're a Strategist, do you have someone who can execute your plan?

NEGATIVE REQUEST

Ask your client this only if you are not getting enough feedback regarding a positive sales experience:

"In order for me to serve you better, please tell me about a negative experience you've had with a salesperson."

The answer defines the type of salesperson your client DOES NOT WANT.

FACILITATOR	MOTIVATOR
• Too pushy, opinionated.	• Had to drag information out of him/her.
• Didn't listen or find out what I really wanted.	• Didn't seem interested in making the sale.
• Wasn't patient.	• Too passive.
• Only interested in results.	• Wouldn't haggle (negotiate).
• Manipulative.	• Didn't get me excited about the deal.
• Too fast.	• Too slow.

Can't you simply discipline yourself to work smart or to work hard? I'm often asked this. The answer is YES, but you will dilute your enthusiasm. You have to count the cost, and the cost could be burnout if you do something you're not designed to do. If the cost is the loss of your passion, it's a heavy cost. For example, it would not be ideal for Strategists to work on a conveyor belt in a fish-gutting factory. They'd have a better chance of remaining enthusiastic and not suffering burnout if they took a supervisory role.

Before the Industrial Revolution, most people didn't have the luxury of questioning whether they were hard-working farmers or Strategist farmers. Since we are totally free to choose, why not search all the possibilities? Why not look to be creative and for opportunities to grow?

You need a selective management system tailored for each work style:

❏ Strategists must have a system of execution (naturally delegate).

❏ Facilitators must have a system of movement (conflicted about delegating).

❏ Motivators must have a system of perspective (don't delegate).

You don't need everything in place to begin working smarter. You can work toward that end. That's why we use the term *wiggling forward*.

CHAPTER 15
YOUR PERSPECTIVE OF TIME
Rhythm

"Humans live in time...therefore...attend chiefly to two things, to eternity itself and to...the Present. For the Present is the point at which time touches eternity...in it alone freedom and actuality are offered."

—C. S. Lewis

In the precious present, we need to be aware of who we are, how we move, and what naturally draws our attention. These things reflect our strengths and disabilities.

Most of us feel that we are being pulled in too many directions. Your nutritionist advises, "If you want to be healthy, follow a simple macrobiotic diet. Boil your rice for five hours a day and prepare dinner using raw foods." Your physical trainer tells you, "You should work out three to four times a week." Your employer requests, "Please join the company baseball team. It only plays once a month." Your son's teacher asks, "Can you help out in the classroom just every other week?" And your family rightfully takes up a lot of your time.

Everyone struggles with time management. It can be a negative subject because of our cultural emphasis on speed and productivity. Time management experts tell us it's easy to manage time and give us practical methods and devices to do so. They offer a one-size-fits-all tool. They try to make time management substantive rather than abstract. The problem is that time is both substantive and abstract.

There are time management tools in every mall in America. But because most people don't have a structural attribute, time management is difficult for them. It eludes their efforts. That's because we try to capture and manage the abstract concept of time as if we were lassoing a steer. Many of us have been told that our lack of organization or lack of self-discipline predisposes us to fail in managing our time well. We surround ourselves with tools to help us solve the problem. We end up with charts, lists, and various time management aids all around us; misused debris mocking our failure with their presence.

I love to walk through a giant office supply store picking up little items and gadgets and clear plastic boxes. I love the idea of being efficient and organized. When a personal organizer came to our home to shape us up, she was shocked to find a section of our closet filled with organizing materials...still wrapped in the original packaging. I have a sincere desire for efficiency, order, and the ability to effectively manage my day...but I did what most other people do, focus on it as an internal failure to be solved only by an external solution or motivator.

To utilize your resources and energy wisely, you have to be effective with your time. And that comes from taking a serious look at how you use and move through time. This is particularly hard to see naturally because it never occurs to us to look at it internally. My aim is help you to consciously inventory how you naturally see, move through and relate to time.

There are four different areas of Time Awareness:

1. Rhythm - Your pace as you move through time.
2. Focus - What you perceive as real, whether it is present moment or bigger picture.
3. Performance - What you actually accomplish on your conveyor belt of time.
4. Energy - Your abstract view of time, whether it has an end for you or is constant and ongoing.

Rhythm is the pace at which you most comfortably move through time. The unique way you apply your dominant abilities is most free and fluid when you move at your own rhythm. As you become aware of your own pace and the pace of those with whom you work and live, you learn how to interact more effectively.

If you were in a plane that was going down, you wouldn't want a Meticulous person as the pilot. He'd take his time being correct, and the plane would crash. You'd want someone who was Expeditious, someone who could move quickly, process information fast and save you. On the other hand, if you needed heart surgery, you wouldn't want an Expeditious surgeon with ten operations scheduled that day.

You'd want your heart surgeon to be Meticulous because his attention to detail could save your life.

We tend to assume that others have the same rhythm as our own. Tempers flare when Meticulous and Rapid people work or play together...or drive on the freeway. Most of us have experienced this: a family is trying to get out the door to an event on time; they're all waiting in the car for the Meticulous person who is still in the house getting ready. Talk about aggravation! This situation needs a Temperate person to keep things under control. When you understand and appreciate natural rhythm, your own and others, your life will get easier at work and at home. Go with the natural rhythm you have. Accept, understand and work with the different natural rhythms of others.

The four rhythms we will discuss are, naturally: Rapid, Meticulous, Temperate and Expeditious.

Rapid people cover a lot of ground quickly. They do everything fast. They're designed to be impatient. Details can be insignificant to them. Because they move quickly, they're apt to make mistakes, but mistakes are not a major concern for them. In fact, movement, action and experience take priority over correctness. Rapid people engage passionately in life.

Do you know someone who is effervescent, exuberant and spontaneous; people who can think quickly on their feet; someone whose fast come-backs make you laugh? Chances are you've encountered individuals who move through time rapidly. Jim Carey and Robin Williams make audiences marvel at the speed of their improvisational humor. Wall Street traders on the Exchange floor quickly handle bids during market fluctuations. The fast-talking auctioneer sees all the bidders and keeps the bids moving. The DJ keeps the party moving. In our fast-paced society, they can help us keep up and adjust.

Rapids easily become frustrated by delays. Waiting patiently seems oppressive to them. Delays make them feel that others are keeping them from accomplishing their goals. Although patience is not natural for them, they need to become aware that most people in their environment do not move, execute, think, or process information as fast as they do. This is an essential point of awareness because they need support from those who do pay attention to detail. It is also important because Rapids love to delegate. They can gift others with leadership and cause others to move into action.

It is essential for them to develop the patience to educate others to their Rapid rhythm. Otherwise, they might be viewed as flighty, frivolous, gruff or irritable. They can display bad temper at anyone who slows them down. Rapid people feel that they are being pulled off the racetrack and forced into an unwanted pit-stop. They can regard the delaying person as an enemy or antagonist, and they can extend that regard to their spouse, children and friends.

Patience is the answer, and Rapid people must reward themselves with spontaneity and play when they manage patience in their lives.

Meticulous people are on the other end of the time spectrum. These individuals are naturally deliberate in moving through time and accomplishing their daily tasks. They are designed to be careful and methodical. The author, Sidney Sheldon, claims that he allows himself twelve rewrites before considering a book ready for his readers. Michelangelo, a Meticulous artist, devoted a full five years to painting and repainting the ceiling of the Sistine Chapel. Examples of Meticulous people in demanding occupations include the Supreme Court Justice who needs exceptional patience to review complicated cases, the engineer who must be thorough in building structures, the heart surgeon, research scientist, editor, and diamond cutter. Our complex world is made up of countless details. Monitoring the details is necessary to its operation and vital to its smooth operation.

Those who are Meticulous have a supreme standard of excellence. They pay painstaking attention to detail and hate to make mistakes. They gift others with thoroughness and elevate the general standard of excellence. When you meet someone who delights in careful accomplishment, deliberates over details of a project, or pauses to weigh a thought or action, you have encountered a Meticulous individual.

Because their rhythm is closely tied to their value system, Meticulous people tend to impose their slow, time-consuming, careful pace on other people, organizations, processes, and environments. While their exacting and methodical approach is usually beneficial, it is not always appropriate. They need to realize that it can be inappropriate and counter-productive. They can spend excessive amounts of time on things that don't require critical excellence...wasting hours, energy and resources. Meticulous individuals must discipline themselves to deliver according to the expectations of others involved. Their own internal standard might well be unrealistic for the situation.

Meticulous persons can get caught up in a complex and damaging spiral which results from an unmanaged fear of imperfection. First, comes the fear of delegating. They're aware that, if they delegate to someone and that person makes a mistake, the silver bullet of blame comes back to strike them. The only way they can delegate is to articulate precisely how they want something done, according to their philosophy. For a Meticulous one to trust, the delegates must also articulate and emulate the Meticulous one's philosophy. The second element of the spiral is fear of themselves making a mistake. This can lead to analysis paralysis. They need to realize that making a mistake is not the end of the world. For a meticulous person to move away from the pain of a mistake, they must learn to regard it as a mid-course correction. Third in the spiral is the fear of being judged. This is the most insidious element because it can be fed secretly by the Meticulous value system. This fear demands that Meticulous persons spend inordinate amounts of time on even the most basic tasks. It confounds their performance and cuts their productivity.

Meticulous individuals can free themselves from these fears

by establishing the needs of their audience and delivering excellence according to those needs...not their own internal standard. This will give them the ability to move forward at a reasonable pace. Also, they must learn to allow others to accomplish tasks in their own styles. It is difficult for Meticulous individuals to do so. They would do well to listen to the words of Mark Twain: "Courage is the resistance to fear, the mastery of fear, and not the absence of fear."

Temperate people adjust their pace to their circumstances. The journalist switches from routine news to a dramatic breaking story; the business leader swings from the crunch of meeting a deadline back to everyday corporate matters; both are Temperate examples. You may not notice them right away because this characteristic focuses on stabilizing rather than creating drama. The person who supports, stabilizes or reassures probably has a Temperate characteristic in their profile. It's not glamorous and usually operates behind the scenes. However, we would remain in constant flux if we didn't have those who place a priority on stability. The nurse, office manager, tax advisor and legal counselor are other good examples. We would be exhausted from the highs and lows of our lives without the stabilizing influence of Temperate people. Former Chief of Staff, now Secretary of State, Colin Powell can easily adjust his pace from a quick strike during a conflict to deliberating over Mid-East peace negotiations. He adjusts his speed to match his environment with stabilization as a primary goal.

Temperate persons are natural regulators with respect to

rhythm. They help Rapid people slow down and work successfully within a group, and they help Meticulous people speed up and catch up with others, accomplish tasks, meet deadlines, and enjoy the process. They want tasks completed in a reasonable amount of time while taking care of details. They have the ability to dance to different rhythms in multiple environments, adjusting appropriately.

> Simply put, when you over-focus on stability you sacrifice creativity and growth.

Temperate rhythm is most sensitive to environment. Temperate individuals need stability in their lives in order to gift others with stability. Without it, they don't have the clarity to carry out their work. If they have to spend vast amounts of energy trying to synchronize with either a Rapid or Meticulous rhythm, they can be derailed. On the other hand, if they dote on stability, they can miss out on opportunities for growth, enjoyment and success. Stability can become an end in itself for them. Simply put, when you overfocus on stability you sacrifice creativity and growth.

They naturally promote balance and stability, and need to engage and educate others from this balanced perspective.

Expeditious people are dedicated to accomplishment, and this determines their rhythm. For them, accomplishment involves getting things done quickly and efficiently, in a way that is noteworthy.

Air traffic controllers must be able to think quickly and simultaneously maintain a high level of quality and precision in their work. The Emergency Room doctor on a busy night moves deftly from one gurney to another, deciding who needs priority treatment. Our fast-paced society needs people who can move quickly while keeping a high standard of excellence. News editors, airline pilots, firefighters, and chefs serve us with expedited excellence.

The ultimate filter question for an Expeditious person is: "Do I want this done fast or do I want this done well?" They must ask themselves that catch-question about everything they do.

Expeditious individuals have limited patience. They are easily frustrated by delays. Waiting patiently seems oppressive to them, making them feel that others are keeping them from accomplishing their goals. Like Rapids, they need to be reminded that most people do not move, perform, think, or process information as fast as they do.

Their desire for fast accomplishment with excellence can generate internal conflict. Unlike Rapids, for them, attention to detail is as important as movement, action and experience. Speed cannot be an excuse for mediocre work.

It is important for them to educate others about their rhythm so they are not perceived as Jekyll-Hyde types when they register frustration at delays.

Meticulous, Temperate and Expeditious are key characteristics. If you have one of these in your profile, it is an essential component of your stability and a point of interaction with all your other attributes.

CHAPTER 16
FOCUS

"The future is something which everyone reaches at the rate of sixty minutes an hour, whatever he does, whoever he is."

—C. S. Lewis

Focus is what a person actually sees. I call it their reality. It is like a camera lens, and there are different lenses for different purposes. Some people are born with a lens that sees the ladybug crawling across a leaf. They see close-up the vivid colors, the brilliance of the micro-world. Others have a zoom lens that moves in to see the ladybug and zooms out to see the leaf, the tree and the park. Still others have a telescopic lens and can see Saturn's rings and the debris inside those rings. The close-up lens that has the acuity to see the ladybug cannot count Saturn's rings. And the telescopic lens that can see Saturn's rings cannot focus on the ladybug. What is real for one person is not apparent to another because they naturally focus on different things.

Do you see the precious present or the bigger picture? Are you aware of your Focus? Because it is a subtle, innate characteristic, most of us are unaware of our Focus. We are also put off or quietly frustrated that others don't see what we see, appreciate what we appreciate, or react in the same way we do.

Specific people continually focus on the present and see things vividly. We all have people in our lives who spontaneously and instantaneously change the mood, inject enthusiasm, display brilliance, and consequently alter the course of a conversation or event. The intuitive person, the existentialist, the person who celebrates living for the precious present, the synergist who shares a brilliant moment of insight - all of these are probably Specific in their focus.

Most of us do not see or celebrate life the way a Specific person does. By continually focusing on the present, they contribute vivid insights. They can be initiators who easily change the focus of a group. Without Specific people, we'd trip over the cracks of life while we were looking at the mountains in the distance. When Rosa Parks refused to sit in the back of the bus, was she planning to alter the course of the civil rights movement? I believe she was only trying to change that moment but it became more. It inspired the entire civil rights movement to build on the momentum she provided.

For those with Specific focus, competence and confidence come from mastering their abilities in the here-and-now. It is difficult for them to set long-term goals. They are controlled by circumstances, and they are more susceptible than most to the tyranny of the urgent and to immediate problems of any magnitude. Because they are easily distracted, they need a lot of help in establishing priorities and maintaining focus. They need to plan the events of their day. It is helpful to list ten things to accomplish for the day and to prioritize them. When diverting things happen during the day, this list will give them a plan and provide the structure they need. And it will keep them from being overwhelmed by diversions, problems and happenstance.

Because they see things so vividly, Specific people must remind themselves that most of their problems aren't as terrible as they seem. Their exaggerated close-up focus makes it difficult for them to gain a true long-range perspective. Therefore, a Specific person needs external support and mechanisms that provide the larger perspective.

By assessing and limiting their distractions, they can remain focused and be more productive.

Spectrum individuals have a balanced focus, and they bring balance to others: their clients, colleagues, family and friends. They have the capability to negotiate the extremes and keep an appropriate focus. The judge, manager, teacher, scientist, and negotiator naturally look for how the present will impact the future. Their balanced viewpoint is essential in moving us from the present into the future.

Since life is about negotiation and Spectrum people are always looking for balance, they represent a touchstone for balance in our own lives. Their participation is especially important in changing environments or situations. As long as they are proactive with respect to change, they can help bring stability and balance to any situation.

Occasionally, their strong desire for balance may paradoxically create a temporary sense of imbalance that can cloud their thinking and immobilize them. If they can determine specifically where they feel out of balance, they can create the systems and structures needed to regain and sustain balance.

Global people have a broad perspective on the whole of life. They live in tomorrow's tomorrow. They gift others with hope and perspective and have the ability to calm or stabilize their peers. They're good at moving themselves and others toward dreams, visions and aspirations.

Where would we be without our visionaries? Economists, sociologists, architects and philosophers have the ability to see the big picture. Martin Luther King, Gandhi and John F. Kennedy all looked beyond the horizon. These people gift us with hope for tomorrow and reassure us about today. They can envision tomorrow's tomorrow while the rest of us vicariously share the enthusiastic hope and comforting reassurance their visions generate. NASA has many Global employees; astronauts literally find their significance living in the future. Judging from the news and the reality programs on television, our society seems to thrive on existential drama. Global people represent a reality check, reminding us of the greater perspective. We need to be reminded about things that will have a long-term impact.

Today can be a nuisance for Global persons...because it's not tomorrow yet. They think in large orbits and land only occasionally. Those with Global focus can easily become frustrated by and disconnected from life's immediate concerns. They're motivated to engage in logistics only if they can see how logistics relate to the big picture. Starting with their dreams, visions, and aspirations for the future and working backward in time, Globals can generate specific action-steps to the present. This helps them remain connected to their goals, by engaging them in the process of actively working toward those goals.

Global people are not easily discouraged. When they are, the discouragement runs deep and has a profound effect on them. When they awfulize their situation, their reality becomes a virtual hell. They're designed to see the world with an eagle eye, soaring above their business and life. Fear can reduce them to the point of losing all sense of perspective. The inability to initiate their dreams creates hopelessness. This in turn creates a resignation that the present discouragement is forever. It becomes an inverted downward spiral.

However, it takes very little for their hope to be renewed. They are encouraged easily if a task at hand has a real and vital connection with one of their dreams or aspirations. They can make the connection by asking themselves, "How will ignoring this issue hinder my pursuit of this goal?" or "How can I pay attention to this issue without hindering the pursuit of my dream?" Global people need systems and structures or the help of others to manage the distracting-but-necessary details of life. This frees them up to begin implementing their aspirations in the here-and-now.

CHAPTER 17
PERFORMANCE

"You can't do it all yourself. Don't be afraid to rely on others to help you accomplish your goals."

—Oprah Winfrey

Performance is what you actually do while time elapses. Some people are designed to start things, to get things moving. Others don't naturally start things, but finish what someone else has started. Some people naturally implement what's already been started. Still others maintain what has been started.

Most people think that they should be able to start, execute, finish and maintain everything they do and do it all well. But that doesn't fit our design. We're designed to specialize. If we spend time trying to do it all ourselves, we reduce our effectiveness. We also reduce our enthusiasm and invite burnout by trying to do what we're not made to do, by going against ourselves.

This area of time awareness is one in which people are always more aware of their weaknesses than their strengths. As with Rhythm and Focus, it is important to celebrate who you are and not spend time thinking about who you're not. There are workable structures and systems to help you in the areas that aren't your natural strengths.

As in all areas of time awareness, to work effectively in a team situation, you must be aware of your own natural Performance style and that of others on your team. That team can be your family, your spouse and yourself, your colleagues at work, or the people to whom you outsource work.

The four kinds of Performance are: Create, Execute, Finalize and Support. Most of us have combinations of these, but no one has them all. They are presented here in the most common combinations.

Create-Execute is a combination exemplified by the instigator, the upbeat morning person, the self-starter and the leader. They get us to move toward next-level growth, creativity and significance. They lead by example, moving first to get us going. They are natural leaders who prompt us to initiate action and projects.

Those with Create-Execute performance traits love to give birth to things, to start things, and to break new ground. Approximately 80% of us are not self-starters. If a Create person was placed in a padded cell for a week with a non-self-starter, the other person would emerge as a lunatic while the Create individual would come out with a host of ideas and numerous plans for initiating any number of things.

Their Execute characteristic means it is natural for them to develop and give shape to any task, project or process that's assigned to them. They want their fingerprints all over the process. They like to design the play, take the ball and run with it.

Since they are Create-Execute, they have no Support or Finalize abilities. They're not designed to maintain what's established or to complete what they begin. Their victory or reward comes at the starting gun, not at the finish line. They are like the chief surgeon who begins the operation and moves quickly to the crucial issues, but depends on others to support and close. Things can get messy and unmanageable for a Create-Execute if they can't put support and closure systems in place. They need help from others to finish and maintain what they have developed. They must set up systems and structures for closure and maintenance or a support team to whom they can delegate these stages.

Create-Finalize persons are those who love to be present at the inception of a project and return to take part in its completion. Inception and fulfillment are the most dramatic and demanding stages of a project, and that's what makes these people respond. The pressure to start or finish projects doesn't intimidate them; they thrive on that pressure.

The marketing director who comes up with the original concept and then reappears for the presentation; the magnate who commissions a ship and shows up with champagne for its launching; the architect who designs a building and checks the workmanship before it's occupied - all are Create-Finalize. They love to create, begin tasks, get contracts signed, get new projects going. They also love to directly impact the process and shape it. They're natural at both beginning and completing jobs, tasks and projects. Their integrity lies in their keen involvement at key stages. They are landscape architects, not gardeners.

Create-Finalize individuals are self-starters, able to move others to action. They possess natural leadership. They're not designed to maintain what they've started. They must have structures and systems of support for implementation and maintenance.

Their Finalize characteristic makes them strong closers. They're proficient at wrapping up loose ends and have the make-up to bring a project to completion.

Since they have no Execute ability, they need to break down assignments and tasks into small units they can easily perform. Here is a simplistic example: Christmas letters for all their business contacts may take a week to write, address and send out. They're frustrated for four days and rewarded on the fifth day when it's done. The solution is to block out small, do-able tasks: *Day 1* - Write the letter; *Day 2* - Get the envelopes; *Day 3* - Get the stamps; *Day 4* - Address the envelopes; *Day 5* - Stuff, stamp and send. They'll be back in the Christmas spirit when they drop the letters through the slot at the post office.

Execute-Finalize is the Performance combination for most people, and we are fortunate for it. Execute-Finalize individuals have the ability to implement what's initiated, and they get the job done. They are the backbone of our society: the fulfiller, contractor, printer and production-line worker. They gift others with productivity. They love to carry a project to completion, to get the task done. It's of chief concern to them that they personally finish what they start.

They're natural at developing and shaping a task, project or process that has been given to them. They like to implement projects and are strong closers, good at wrapping up loose ends, with the drive to bring a project to completion.

They require external pressure in order to get started, and they need systems and structures to maintain what has been established. They're not procrastinators by nature, though they may think they are. They don't put things off intentionally; they simply aren't natural self-starters. They need to be pressured to get the ball rolling. If a guest is coming for dinner, that's their pressure point to clean the house. If they have an exam at school tomorrow, that provides the impetus to study.

With no Support ability, they're not designed to maintain what they've established. Again, they need to employ systems and structures that help them maintain, or they must have a support team to whom they can delegate.

Execute-Support people find their significance in helping you find your significance. You'll have to look behind the green curtain to find the ones who hold it all together: personal assistant, wedding planner, office manager, and consummate homemaker. They don't need to be in front or at the center. Their confidence is strongest when they work with a strong, effective leader. Della Street and Perry Mason come to mind.

They are comfortable in necessary, but not necessarily glamorous, jobs. Unobtrusively, they play pivotal roles in our lives. They are loyal and tenacious, supporting a project once it's been delegated to them. Their strength is endurance.

Having the Execute ability, they are natural at developing and giving shape to an assigned task, project or process. They enjoy implementing, once they get started. They can be resistant to change.

Because of their Support characteristic, they are natural facilitators. Their significance and reward come in maintaining what has been established or created. It's a crucial role because they're gifted in ways that a large number of people are not.

They are without Create or Finalize abilities. Since they have no Create characteristic, they have a hard time getting started. They need pressure to get going. They have to be given specific tasks and encouragement when they start. They must set up support structures to provide starting pressure-points. Since they have no Finalize ability, they also need deadlines or other incentives to bring things to completion. Their focus and reward are not at the finish line or in the limelight.

I believe Execute-Support people display a quiet nobility in being able to find their significance in what they do, rather than how they are lauded. It is a remarkable form of independence. A dynamic leader is fortunate to have an advocate who enjoys projects delegated to them and one who tenaciously holds down the fort. They facilitate others to move forward because they provide support and peace of mind to those around them. Many people make a living by what they get. Those gifted with Execute and Support make a life by what they give.

CHAPTER 18
ENERGY

"Trust only movement. Life happens at the level of events, not of words. Trust movement."

—Alfred Adler

This area of time awareness is filled with nuance...with the abstract, aesthetic part of time...with the invisible. Therefore, it is the hardest to identify and describe. It's like the breeze we feel across our face but cannot see, touch or hold. In a sense it touches us. It is noticeable through the results and consequences of its presence rather than by appearance.

Energy is the area where we must celebrate movement, closure, achievement or results with positive experiences. For each style, this means taking a lap of honor around the track after the race is run. We frequently forget to do that and simply move on to the next race. It is vital to create an experience of rest and rejuvenation. The play, rest and relaxation, and enjoyment of life must match the work. In this way, we memorialize our small successes and remind ourselves of what we've accomplished. Rest, play and relax-ation prevent burnout. These joys re-engage and reinforce good behavior while rejuvenating us, so we're ready for the next race. Refreshed and ready, we can move forward to a higher level of efficiency and effectiveness. Without celebration, we develop environmental and relational toxins that rob us of our joy.

Henri Amiel says, "Without passion man is a mere latent force and possibility, like the flint which awaits the shock of the iron before it can give forth it's spark."

Initially, it is difficult to identify what energizes us or touches our consciousness inside time. However, once you identify and own it, it can buoy your enthusiasm, prevent burnout and create positive experiences in the form of either islands of remembrance or celebrations of pragmatic results. So, although subtle, your Energy style can have a substantial impact on you.

This is one of the top five areas where communication breaks down between spouses, parent and child, or boss and employee. The other four areas are: Core Nature, Learning Style, Rhythm, and Focus. It is also a major cause of burnout when misused: he never stops; she has a short attention span; he pushes too hard to get it done; he's always starting new things and never finishing them.

I met a wife married to the same man for thirty years. She's still waiting for her perpetually-in-motion husband to stop and rest in the evenings and on weekends. Due to his Energy style, this will never happen. This is another case where we can miss the mark because we believe we can get the other person to change and be like us. We like to think that the person who naturally moves from event to event to event will miraculously change and learn to celebrate, rest and rejuvenate; that the person who loves to continually start things will transform to focus on getting things finished. It's not going to happen! The person who is disjointed, jumping from subject to subject to subject will change to be efficient, linear and logical. No way! When we expect miraculous transformations, we set ourselves up to be disappointed...with each other and ourselves.

This area of time awareness holds many positive aspects and benefits for us. There are four Energy styles: Perpetual, Finite, Periodic and Catalytic.

Perpetual people can work until 4:00 am and be back in the office, showered and fresh, four hours later. Others work late and drag in at 10:00 am, hardly able to function. Boundless energy comes to mind when it comes to Perpetual people. Many celebrities who live and perform in multiple time zones perform with high energy and enthusiasm. It doesn't bother them to be in New York on Monday and Rome on Tuesday. They don't see time, and so the obstacles that time represents are not hindrances. Those who are Perpetual insist that society move forward or at least move. They do not sit on their hands, and they motivate others to keep moving.

As I said a few sentences ago, Perpetual people do not naturally see time; instead, they see events in time, moving in a perpetual motion from one event to the next. They experience closure as the completion of a task or reaching exhaustion. This makes them exceptionally tenacious, unwilling to give up or end a task prematurely. Natural break-points do not occur to them. Breaks for eating regularly or stopping to celebrate a finished achievement are not on their agenda. This can lead to physical or emotional burnout.

They must schedule breaks for themselves and develop the discipline to take them for the sake of their health, relationships and work quality. Some clients set timers or program their computers to generate messages as ways of reminding themselves to take a break. Because they don't naturally see time, they have no problem sacrificing it. Though they seem to have boundless energy, perpetual people are prone to burnout. They view themselves as superhuman in regard to any task, and they will pour themselves into a project with complete disregard for their health, family and other needs. I remind them to take a break. Long-distance swimmers know that they must take a breath with every stroke to swim a mile. If they don't, they won't make it.

It is vital for Perpetual individuals to realize that play must balance work. They are not superhuman and need replenishment and rejuvenation as much as anyone. They must schedule perpetual down-times; periods of rest and rejuvenation, vacations, or weekends away. They need to create systems and structures for balance. For them, balance means folding play into their continuous activities.

Finite people experience closure in terms of order, decorum, natural law, traditional measurements of time, or other predetermined disciplines. They are generally extremely aware of sunrises, sunsets, seasons, clocks, calendars, and significant dates. They instinctively know when to be done.

Others may meander through time, but those who are Finite focus on the end result. And they focus so intently that they gift closure to those who can't finish projects easily. The auctioneer, accountant, salesman and clock-watcher each have finite amounts of sand in their hourglasses. At a dinner party with friends, have you ever noticed it's always the same person who winds the evening down? Chances are, your friend is Finite. I have a friend who half-jokes, "You've been a guest in my house long enough." when he wants us to go home.

Because of their preferences for natural and traditional order, it is essential for Finite people to celebrate and rejuvenate according to natural and traditional order. They must rest at the end of the day and at the end of the week, celebrate special days and holidays and celebrate the seasons. They are steeped in traditional observances and schedules.

For them, the completion of major projects is important. Finite people love the sense of closure. They begin everything they do with the end in mind. When their sense of closure is disrupted, frustration and paralysis set in. They need to measure their accomplishments with positive milestones. Using a tool such as a day-planner or making a list of positive possibilities can be helpful.

Periodic persons experience time in terms of the events and tasks that are occurring right now. They can carry out many tasks at the same time and have a natural ability to come back to ongoing projects without interrupting flow. They can suspend a sense of closure indefinitely while they are compelled to perform the next task or enter into the next event that presents itself. Consequently, it is important that Periodics develop the discipline of refusing to take on many simultaneous projects. Accepting too many tasks makes the completion of any task doubly difficult. Periodic individuals need a regular way to discharge the information and events they've been involved in. Think of it as a brain shunt to relieve the pressure. It is also essential for them to become single-minded when it comes to high-priority events or tasks.

Air traffic controllers, stockbrokers and short-order cooks all need the natural or learned ability to multi-task. They must be able to keep a vast amount of information straight and immediately available for action or assimilation. My nickname is the Nutty Professor because I've been known to jump from one subject to another and back again. I'm often told it's quite a ride for those on the other side of the conversation. Hey! My style is Periodic...What can I say? I believe this ability enables me to retain and access the information I need when I review the profiles of many individuals. Periodic people can recall data in their memories with remarkable speed.

Periodics are sensitive to environment. Without discipline, they may have difficulty completing any task. They can become over-stimulated and overloaded, causing fatigue, frustration and burnout. It is essential that they celebrate the achievement of their milestones. Because they are able to multi-task, seasoning their work environment with play and other refreshing activities will serve to rejuvenate them. Without celebration, they may develop environmental and relational toxins that will rob them of their energy and enthusiasm.

To achieve balance in their lives, they must create systems and structures for follow-through and for rejuvenation.

Catalytic people are compelled to see things begin. They are designed to experience time in terms of the events and tasks that have not yet happened, but need to occur in order to provide momentum for subsequent events. For Catalytics, the energy created by beginning a task or project translates into immediate ultimate success or failure.

The writer, inventor, and artist are representative Catalytic people. Where we keep one journal to express our thoughts, they've started twenty-eight different journals. While others focus on the finish line, they search for the next opportunity to begin. Most of us go into semi-retirement after a big accomplishment. Catalytic people insist on going to the next creative pursuit. They feed us our next endeavor. They give us the gift of inspiration and fill any void with creativity.

They are the instigators in our lives. For instance, if they open the refrigerator and find eggs, they begin breakfast. This creates momentum for getting to work which in turn creates the momentum for getting their work done, getting home, having a good time with their spouse and kids, and so forth. However, if the eggs aren't in the refrigerator, a breakdown in the entire sequence can occur. Catalytics search desperately for other things they might begin successfully, piling up one uncompleted task after another. If they're not careful, they can become completely buried in initiating tasks and events, leading to frustration and feeling overwhelmed.

They have the ability to create change and to provide the initial momentum for tasks and projects. They use multiple opportunities as the catalyst to get things moving. They remind others of the satisfaction associated with getting things started.

Catalytics require self-discipline to make sure the tasks they've begun reach completion. They must learn not to panic if things don't begin the way they intended...and not to easily abandon one project for the sake of another. They need to create systems and structures for balance, including a mechanism for follow-through on what they've started as well as time for play, rest and relaxation.

CHAPTER 19
SIGNIFICANT SOCIAL ENVIRONMENT

"The art of conversation is the art of hearing as well as of being heard."

—William Hazlitt

Everyone has a "people fuel tank" which holds their fuel for engaging in social interaction. Some people have a tank that can hold 55 gallons of people fuel. Others are designed with a very small tank that holds at most 5 gallons of people fuel. Because people are designed differently, we need to appreciate and accommodate those differences. We can't assume that everyone has the average 23 gallons of people fuel. What's too much social interaction for one may be just right or too little for another.

Introspective individuals are not being hostile when they want some time alone; they are simply evidencing their design to enjoy their own company. They are made to rejuvenate inside themselves. When they do that, they're more receptive to human interaction. Conversely, it is not unusual if a Gregarious person never wants to be alone; they're designed to thrive and revive with the stimulation of people, around noise, next to other human heartbeats.

At an office party, you can spot a Gregarious colleague who bounces from one person to another. You'll have to look a little harder, but you'll see an Introspective colleague who gets with one person and spends the entire party engaging in a one-on-one stimulating conversation.

Here, you need to schedule your week around your design. If you're a private person, carve out time for intro-spection. If you're a Gregarious person, surround yourself with friends who champion you and with whom you can play, grow, rest, feel safe, clarify, and interact.

Your Significant Social Environment is where you find your greatest freedom, safety and rewards in life. It's where your unique abilities are best clarified, evaluated and refreshed. When you inventory this area of your life, the question to ask yourself is: "Am I getting the people time or private time I need to rejuvenate, restore my enthusiasm, and prevent burnout?" These benefits are important.

Of course, there are many different capacities and situa-tions. Investigate to gauge your capacity, and relate it to your living style. Questions to ask yourself include: Are my relationships toxic for me? Are they moving me forward? Do I have balance in this area? Am I too withdrawn? Am I at every party, but not getting anything done? It's worthwhile asking these filter questions to create awareness and clari-ty in this area of your life.

As a sad example, I had an Introspective client who cre-ated very little time to rejuvenate herself. When I asked about her significant relationships, she replied that she was allergic to her friends. Initially, I thought it was a bizarre statement. Then, I realized that, as an Introspective woman, she hadn't celebrated her introspection and created an environment for it. Therefore, she resented her friends for depriving her of much-needed private time.

Whether you are Introspective, Gregarious, or Introspective-Relational, it's worth repeating that no ability operates in a vacuum. It is possible to be a truly Introspective person and yet have one or more relational abilities. And this can cause internal conflict. You may feel you need your own company and yet you also need the company of others occasionally. You're truly Introspective, but you like people and like to help others. That's very natural. Similarly, you may be a Gregarious person and have a learning style that requires you to remove yourself from distractions.

The key to determining your Significant Social Environment is determining what environment allows you to rejuvenate.

Introspective individuals value their time alone. They're motivated to designate significant time for personal reflection and meditation. They're designed to enjoy their own company with a few close friends. It's important that they allow themselves time to reflect and create a heightened perspective of their work and life. They're at home in their private world and don't tend to feel isolated or lonely when working alone.

They need their private space and time. It's in their best interests to have a place of refuge where they can escape on a regular basis from people-related demands. They're able to contribute clarity and insight when they maintain this private sanctuary. Without it, their relationships and world become toxic for them. They must carve out private time in their daily and weekly schedules.

They need a work environment that permits private space and regular intervals of private time so they can refuel their people tank.

Introspective-Relational people are ideally suited for people-saturated, service-driven industries. They come to life when they're around people. They only require a small amount of private time to refuel their energies and process their own thoughts.

Because they revive around people, they need to remain focused relationally rather than on projects. They atrophy emotionally without a goodly amount of people interaction. They find significance in both private and public time, so they need to balance the two. They gain clarity both by having meaningful encounters with others and by spending time alone. Without maintaining a balance, they may become disoriented. Introspective-Relational people can become toxic if they do not spend meaningful private time.

Gregarious individuals thrive and revive around other people, lots of people. They are in heaven in a crowded room. Without lots of people interaction, they can become depressed. It is important that their work and play involve interaction with many people. They value time spent with others and are motivated by relationships, social events, and other highly relational activities. They work well in environments requiring interaction and contribute warmth, humor and vitality.

If called on to work by themselves, they may get bored easily and find inappropriate ways to socialize. They must find appropriate times for socializing and make the most of those opportunities. They need to remember that life does not consist entirely of socializing and that they must get down to work occasionally.

They gain clarity and perspective when they interact with people. They need meaningful social events and activities. If they don't schedule regular people times, life may become stale for them. Regularly rewarding themselves with social events, parties, and gatherings will keep them energized.

It is a mistake to assume that people-lovers can't burnout on people. They must reduce exposure to anyone toxic for them, such as fearful or complaining clients or colleagues. To protect against people burnout, they must socialize with friends who aren't business-related. Depression negatively impacts their interactions and sphere of influence. To counteract it, they can consciously choose to be around positive people.

How does your Significant Social Environment affect relationships? Again, we're back to awareness of who you are and with whom you're in a relationship. This applies professionally and personally. *You're not going to get others to change to be like you.* People in good relationships learn to negotiate, and vice versa. My wife is Introspective and I'm Gregarious. We've negotiated in our relationship to take two cars to a party. Joan says hello, visits an hour or two, and says goodbye. I close the party down. When she's done socializing, she leaves in her car, and I leave much later in mine. And it's okay because we know each other's needs and have learned to accommodate. On Saturday morning, we may have breakfast together; I am dismissed for the day; and she goes to walk the dogs or work on crafts.

One person's style in this area can be threatening to another. For some undefinable reason, it can undermine a sense of safety or stability simply by being what it is. My Introspective wife can feel that my open invitation for friends to pop by is intrusive. We have a revolving front door on our home. For her, it dilutes the intimacy and connection to host a large group. Another of our negotiations: whatever home we live in must have a large master bedroom to which she can retreat. When I want to talk to someone until 2:00 am or when I have twenty family members over for a game night, she needs a place of refuge.

As a Gregarious person, sometimes I feel thwarted by her introspection. I may plan to go out with my movie club; if we haven't negotiated this, she may say, "I wanted us to stay home tonight." I may feel a bit ambushed because, as a Gregarious person, I generally relax and have more fun in a group dynamic. It brings out the best in me. Negotiation is highly personal and requires constant attention.

Ability management is proactive. It's working and living smart, not hard. If you're surrounded by people at work and you're Introspective, you need to inject private time into your world, like doses of vitamins. If you're Gregarious and you're isolated at work, you need social engagements to look forward to: lunches, movie clubs, whatever. But in your daily life, it is important that your social significance is honored. In this balance, you are mastering the simple and the subtle aspects of your nature.

CHAPTER 20
CORE NATURE

"All I would tell people is to hold on to what was individual about themselves, not to allow their ambition for success to cause them to try to imitate the success of others. You've got to find it on your own terms."

—Harrison Ford

Your core nature is what attaches meaning to relationships, vocation, actions and experiences. It's your significance filter. What's meaningful or significant to you may completely elude someone else's filter. It includes what you value most and seek most from interpersonal communication and other processes. It is your reward system, determining how your unique abilities are best clarified, evaluated and refreshed. A person's core nature is either Aesthetic or Pragmatic, very rarely both.

Your Core Nature governs two major functions: (1) receiving and inventorying communication, experiences, environments, relationships, and movement; and then (2) acting on the information processed by executing a milestone or creating an experience.

From an ability management standpoint, if the soul has a home, this is where it resides.

Aesthetics focus on experiences, feelings, tone and words. They become aware of context before they focus on content, seeking out a pattern or rhythm of events or information. They value the impact of words, preferring to be told rather than shown how they are appreciated.

They tend to have more freedom than Pragmatics since they are not tied to material or monetary rewards. They regard money primarily as a means to positive life experiences and memories.

Aesthetics are keen at evaluating people, events, environments and organizations. They bring humanity into a project or situation. Their nurturing and relational nature is what draws others to them. They are sensitive to criticism because they hear the "Ouch" before the content of the statement. They often give up tangible rewards in exchange for verbal praise. If they can't manage this ability, they may have to settle for being liked rather than respected.

Aesthetics need appreciation for being good parents, spouses, or professionals. Notice, acknowledgement and validation with meaningful words feed their soul. They'll hold onto words and the thoughts behind the words as signs of true appreciation. They tend to nurture others with words, affirmations and subtle gestures.

They may assume that everyone else processes information and establishes goals and rewards in the same way they do. This can lead to value blindness. Their competence and confidence come from having safe or supportive, non-judgmental environments and relationships. They need to educate others who do not share the same rewards and values as to what they find rewarding.

The way to motivate an Aesthetic is with words of appreciation rather than deadlines or milestones. They need to feel championed. It creates a non-critical nurturing environment, which allows them to clarify and act on that clarity.

Natural predators for Aesthetics are environments and situations in which productivity is valued higher than human or poetic considerations. Environments promoting criticism become toxic for them.

They need to reward themselves with life experiences, islands of remembrance. They must be rich in life experiences. The consequence of not achieving this will be burnout.

Aesthetic is a key characteristic. If you are Aesthetic, it is an essential component of your stability and a point of interaction with all your other attributes.

Pragmatics focus on results as tangible milestones. They zero in on content first, then context. They constantly want to know when, how much, where, who and why. They regard actions and material rewards as signs of appreciation.

They regard money as stored energy, seeing financial assets as stability and resources for positive action...new and more results. Material acquisitions nurture their sense of significance. They are results-oriented and strong at evaluation for substantive achievement.

Pragmatics generally evaluate progress and communication on the basis of concrete substance and down-to-earth reality. They believe the facts. Their attitude is: show me that you care by what you do, not by what you say. They need to know the Why to be affirmed. Why am I a good professional/parent/spouse? They need to be seen, acknowledged and validated with substance.

They may assume that everyone else processes information and establishes goals and rewards the same way they do. Again, this can lead to value blindness. Pragmatics are not motivated by words and can be insensitive to those who are. They might be considered materialistic and harsh if they don't manage this ability.

Their competence and confidence come from results, accomplishments, achievements and significant actions. They're motivated by the real, the tangible, and the practical. They are impacted by the written statement...bank statements, graphs, written goals, journals...anything that transfers a goal from their heads to a substantive reality.

They accept criticism more effectively than Aesthetics because they focus more on the content than on the nuance of the criticism. They accept and use criticism positively to move forward.

Pragmatics must educate others who do not share the same rewards and values as to what rewards them. The way to motivate them is with milestones, not nurturing words.

They need to acknowledge a job well done with substantial rewards...a vacation, a new set of golf clubs, a new suit, or anything else of value to them. The consequence of not rewarding themselves is burnout.

Relationships between Aesthetics and Pragmatics. Most couples have opposing core natures, and these are not gender-specific. When a husband and wife watch *The Antiques Road Show* on television, they think they're enjoying a shared experience. And they are, except it's not the same experience. For example, if a woman presents a beautiful painting inherited from her family, as the appraiser shares his expertise, the wife and husband each hear differently. If the wife is an Aesthetic, she hears: "17th-Century original oil painting by a Flemish artist; passed down from her great grandmother; wants to pass this heirloom down to her daughter; priceless; I'd never part with it!" Her Pragmatic husband hears: "It's really old. Worth $36,000; it would pay for the addition above the garage; I wonder if she'd agree to sell it?"

An historic example of how abilities are not gender-specific is presented by Caesar and Cleopatra. Caesar was Aesthetic. He was wounded more by the emotional betrayal of his friend Brutus than by being actually stabbed in the back. His last words were, "Et tu, Brutus?" Cleopatra was Pragmatic. She focused on acquisitions and was able to regain all the land lost by previous pharaohs. She was also a formidable strategist.

When it comes to purchasing a home, Aesthetics will

focus on creating a nesting environment. Pragmatics will zero in on the money and on the practicalities of acquisition in a prestigious neighborhood with good schools.

This is an area of great misunderstanding in relationships. If you know your own Core Nature, it will help you communicate to others what you need from them. When two people in a significant relationship learn to tell each other their needs, concerns, fears and frustrations, it can go a long way to promoting harmony. Because partners generally differ in their Core Natures, a good question is: "Am I loving my partner the way he or she needs to be loved...not the way I need to be loved?" My wife is Aesthetic, so it is important to her that I tell her I love and appreciate her. Since I am Pragmatic, it is important to me that she shows me she loves me by her actions.

These principles also apply in business and social relationships. An effective way to avoid miscommunication and bring clarity to a discussion is to mirror back what was understood. "What I'm hearing you say is........." That gives the other person an opportunity to correct or to affirm that you got it. If you're not at all sure what the other person said, ask "Can you tell me that in another way?"

In my favorite movie *It's a Wonderful Life*, we have great examples of the Pragmatic and Aesthetic in action. George is Pragmatic. Mary is Aesthetic. In one memorable scene, after George has given away their honeymoon money to save the Building & Loan, he is squired to a dilapidated house. His disgust with the place is evident on his face as he enters. But his face brightens when he sees the tangible things Mary has done to create a honeymoon suite with homey fire, a roasting chicken, travel posters, cozy curtains and bedding. Mary becomes the center of attention. She carefully created a honeymoon setting that for her may as well have been in the Waldorf Astoria. She created a memory with George. Her face beams. Both are pleased and rewarded for different reasons.

One further complication to this area is that every ability has its own profile. A person can be Aesthetic, but also have one or more abilities that tend to be Pragmatic, such as Justice. Although you are Aesthetic, your pragmatism comes out when your Justice ability is engaged. A person can be Pragmatic with a very Aesthetic ability like Nurturer. In either case, some of your attributes may balance out your Core Nature. Alternatively, you may be Pragmatic with one or more attributes that are also strongly Pragmatic, intensifying your Pragmatic Core Nature. Because of these complexities, you may identify somewhat with both Aesthetic and Pragmatic, but remember...you're looking for the dominant Core Nature.

When I review a client's profile, the first thing I note is whether they are Aesthetic or Pragmatic because it affects the entire direction of the consultation. If you're going to master being yourself, it is essential that you identify your Core Nature.

CHAPTER 21
DISCOVERING WHERE YOU ARE

"Everyone who got where he is had to begin where he was."

—Robert Louis Stevenson

In previous chapters, we provided information on inventorying your innate abilities and how you naturally use them. In this chapter, you will inventory where you currently find yourself, how you talk to yourself, and how your environment affects you.

Although people don't change, their environment and circumstances can. And you have the power to change your environment and circumstances. You also have the power to change your internal monologue and significantly impact your life.

Once you know your design and recognize the environment you need to thrive, the next step is to start consciously creating that optimal environment for yourself. If you've discovered from your ability inventory that you are an orchid, you must begin building a greenhouse to meet your needs.

Some people I profile are orchids attempting to survive in the desert. Some declare that they don't deserve a greenhouse or they'll build one later...or they'll create a green-house for themselves after they build greenhouses for everyone else. Instead of moving toward their most benefi-cial environment, they sabotage their own growth and suc-cess, believing it nobly self-sacrificing to deny themselves. In reality, only by accepting their design and working with it can they experience the success they were meant to have.

I recall talking with a woman who had a nicely balanced profile. It wasn't edgy or dramatic; it was stable. In review-ing her profile with her, there weren't many obstacles to address because she was doing well. While it is likely she will never be an extraordinary standard bearer, she is blessed with an extraordinary contentment in her pursuits and circumstances.

Her example brought home to me that the more people are gifted, the more they are challenged. Consider the artis-tic community, comprised of people who have a great capacity for creativity and growth. These same people can also suffer great angst and become overpowered by it. Many end up isolated, lonely, disenchanted and worse.

Whether you are an orchid or a cactus, you are awe-somely and wonderfully made, and your design comes with its own blessings and challenges.

Have a conversation with yourself. To effectively man-age your abilities, you must first learn how to hold an ongoing conversation with yourself regarding your abilities. By bring-ing into play the different facets of who you are, you can create the consistency and balance your profile needs. Learning which of your attributes to use in any given situation will enable you to stand in the center of your significance.

I train people to have positive conversations with themselves about their innate abilities. In these conversations, I urge them to be truthful, positive, gracious, and practical.

I go back to the metaphor of your abilities being like the white Arabian stallions in Ben Hur. You must make sure that you control the reins, that your abilities are positioned correctly and moving in unison, the way they're designed to move. It requires constant maintenance and management and conversation with yourself.

In a sense, with this ongoing conversation you are parenting yourself positively. By learning to nurture yourself, you gift yourself with the positive movement, peace of mind, safety and security that you need to move toward the success and significance you are designed for. *By accepting joyfully your childlike qualities and gifting others with your mature abilities, you can experience joyful significance.* The blending of all your attributes is required for you to gain optimum significance.

Before you can effectively converse with anyone else about your abilities, you must first gain an understanding and perspective of them yourself. If you haven't talked with yourself about your abilities and arranged them in your mind, you leave yourself open to communication problems. In relationships, not articulating your needs sets up other people to disappoint or frustrate you because you expect them to guess your needs. They inadvertently trigger security and momentum issues that are important to you. Your effectiveness is diminished before you can have a conversation with them about their needs.

Many individuals who have strong nurturing characteristics are not nurturing toward themselves. Their internal conversation with and about themselves is driving, non-relational, ungracious, unforgiving and relentless.

During a tour of Israel, on the road to Emmaus, we stopped near a giant ravine. On the far side of the ravine walked a boy shrouded in black from head to toe. He made his way along a steep slope with all the sheep following behind. It was an ancient scene to which our professor added some perspective. In ancient times, you could identify a shepherd because his flock would follow him anywhere. You could also identify a butcher...because the butcher wouldn't have the shepherd's nurturing relationship with the flock, the sheep wouldn't follow him. So the butcher had to take a long stick and drive them to market to be butchered. In the natural use of our abilities, we can nurture other people and butcher ourselves without being conscious of it.

Actively listen in conversation with others. Just as you actively listen for what's going on inside you, use active listening techniques to filter what is being said by others and to hear the true need behind their words or tones.

A woman sounded upbeat and excited during her profile interview. She was in her forties with four children. What she shared about her health didn't fit. She'd recently been told she had only ninety days to live. An aggressive form of cancer had invaded her organs. You would never have known it from her voice. She was a Nurturer, Aesthetic and an Engineer. She had followed these rules: toughen up, be less outgoing, and don't be an artist. When I spoke to her on the phone at the start of her profile review, she tried to be upbeat and optimistic with me. I told her I was "looking forward to addressing where your rage and anger come from." There was a long silence at the other end.

Then she said, "I'm not angry, I'm not full of rage."

I replied, "Well, depression can be anger turned inwards. And cancer can be swallowed fury, so I wonder where is this coming from?"

And she answered, "Well, I'm not angry about anything." Ten minutes into our conversation, her tears were flowing freely.

Until then, she hadn't been given permission to be angry. Growing up, she'd learned that it wasn't appropriate for her to get angry. Others in her family who expressed their anger inappropriately were negative models for her. As a Nurturer, she believed she was supposed to be a model of good behavior. To her, that meant being absolutely optimistic about her cancer. Everyone in her family was caught up in the tragedy of a young mother about to die. I looked past it to concern myself with her living moments and the cause of her fury.

When she hung up the phone after getting some of her anger out, she had hope because she had a plan, whether she lived or died. If she lived, she planned to be a model of thriving. And if she died, she planned to leave a legacy for her children as a model of thriving in adversity.

Her kids were teenagers and joked with her. She had permitted them only to be upbeat and positive. They were not allowed to be confused, angry or afraid. Her husband, a quiet man, was grieving. I told her she needed to write him a letter telling him not to revert to being withdrawn without her. She needed to write to her kids about her wishes, hopes and dreams for them. I told her she had to bring her true feelings to the surface and obtain closure.

The Pollyanna attitude she'd adopted accomplished nothing. It simply passed on the generational sin of pretending to be perfect. It masked her true grief and anger and would cause it's own grief in the future.

Learn to listen for what's behind what others say. It will enable you to tap into their needs, concerns, fears and frustrations and relate to others in a deeper, more meaningful way.

Engage in conversation with the Creator. This is an important but often overlooked conversation. It trips up a lot of people, but when we learn how to have this conversation, it connects us to the greater purposes and eternal truths that touch our lives.

There is a story of Jesus surrounded by a group of adults. Children standing behind the adults couldn't get through to see Jesus. The adults believed the children shouldn't be allowed to bother Him and prevented them from coming forward. But Jesus said, "Let the little children come to me." He invited the children to come play, visit, sit on his lap, and snuggle. We adults often miss the mark in our conversations with our Creator. When adults hear Jesus' invitation, their reaction is: "Let me go get cleaned up. Let me put on my best clothes. Let me learn some Hebrew or Latin so I can converse effectively. Let me get a holy mat so when I sit on his lap, I won't smudge it up. I won't look Him in the eye, and I'll only speak when I'm spoken to." That's quite different than the children's natural, joyful, immediate response.

We may be overwhelmed, distracted, frustrated, bitter or angry. Coming into conversation with our Creator that way can distort, devalue or deny our intention. Our thoughts are that we're not good enough, that we're too messed up. The wall of guilt and justification we put up can sever true communication with our Creator.

It's fear in the form of the hissing snake again...and getting ready to get ready without acting or moving. The answer is movement. Our adult self must step aside and let the child within each of us come, engage and receive.

What is your purpose on this planet? Here is the key to ultimate significance, full enthusiasm, full safety, full blessing! This is the area of mirroring back your creation to your Creator.

I met and profiled a young man who was enthusiastic and unusually wise for his age. Over the next few years, he embraced his profile and demonstrated his ability to practically apply what he learned to various aspects of his life. As he matured and succeeded in his life, he developed sophisticated problems. He had married, established himself financially, and purchased a vacation home at a resort while still a young man. Then he discovered that he was bored by life. His wife's grandmother died, and he was asked to serve as pallbearer. Although he hardly knew the grandmother, the experience had a profound effect on him. At the funeral home, he was confronted with an open casket containing the woman's body. It triggered him to think about life and death, and life beyond death. The question hung in his mind: Is that all there is? The more he thought about it, the more hopeless he felt. He contemplated his own life, decades more of making money, continuing relationships, and the Why of it all.

His reticular activator had been turned on. Later, he walked into the family living room while his mother and his aunt were watching *The Jerry Springer Show.* The program was about a mother who'd been sleeping with her daughter's boyfriend. It prompted him to consider the existence of evil. His parents were atheists, and he had never been taught the concept of evil. He occasionally went to church, but disliked the restrictions and deleted it from his life. He had grown well in every regard except in his conversation with his Creator. From despair and hopelessness, he decided to seek a way to fill that void.

I discussed with him how he could engage in conversation with his Creator and locate a spiritual environment that would fit him. I told him to find a church where people with questions can feel comfortable asking them. To go where he could wear shorts and sandals and be accepted. I described how a Free Spirit has to engage. I gave him specific books and articles to read. He now enthusiastically embraces the Faith he has chosen. His success in business is now only part of a bigger picture for him.

If you haven't already done so, I encourage you to find and name your Higher Power. A conversation with an inanimate, vague and arbitrary Creator isn't likely to be meaningful or beneficial.

Put yourself in a championing environment. We all need someone to champion us. Who is championing you? How are they championing you? When coaches review a client's profile, I ask them, "What kind of coaching environment does your client need?" This can vary greatly from one person to another. One client needs a safe place where they can be vulnerable; another needs an environment for brainstorming and synergy; one requires a place to find clarity; another needs an environment where growth can be inventoried and celebrated; still another needs a place of balance between responsibility and freedom. Choose the environment or environments you would want and share your selection with one of your personal champions.

It is important to surround yourself with others who want to grow and move forward in their lives. For quite a while, I was involved with a close-knit group that worked well together on creative projects I found rewarding. We had fun together, and members of the group were warm and supportive. However, after a while, I noticed that most people in this group were more interested in commiserating about their difficulties than in finding solutions and moving forward. They effectively encouraged each other to remain stuck in place, and it virtually became the group glue that everyone shared, being miserable. I decided to distance myself from them and spend time with others who shared my desire for growth. If you find yourself in a similar situation, you'll need to make some decisions and changes to move forward in your life.

CHAPTER 22
RELATIONSHIP DYNAMICS

"We cannot live only for ourselves. A thousand fibers connect us with our fellow men."

—Herman Melville

Thermostats and Thermometers. In every personal and professional relationship, there is a thermostat and a thermometer. The thermostat regulates the temperature, and the thermometer reads the temperature. The thermostat is that member of the relationship whose natural abilities set or change the emotional temperature of the environment, determining calm or urgency, joy or distress.

The thermometer is that individual who responds to the temperature set and any changes in temperature. The thermometer asks, "Do I wear a sweater or a tee shirt in this relationship today?"

In any relationship...business partners, father and daughter, husband and wife...the one who is the thermostat and the other who is the thermometer remain constant. Exceptions to this are rare. The designated roles are not gender-specific. This is an area of relationship that can be misread easily.

Husbands and wives are good examples. An easy way to distinguish the thermostat from the thermometer is to observe what happens when a husband or wife enters the house for the evening. The first five minutes of interplay, conversation or the lack thereof literally sets the tone for the entire evening. One sets it; the other reads it and responds.

A proper question is: Who sets the tone in the relationship? Additional questions are: What is the one major area that triggers a temperature change? Is it impatience? Frustration? Anger? Hurt? Feeling overwhelmed? What is the pattern? What is the chief cause of change?

My wife and I are excellent examples. Joan is bright, educated, cerebral, and spends a lot of time in her head. I'm hotheaded and emotional, a sparkplug. But things are not what they seem. My wife is the thermostat, and I am the thermometer. Because I'm verbal, the mouthpiece in the family, most people would assume I'm the thermostat. In reality, my wife is. She has some intense attributes and her mind-set determines the tone for the day.

Thermometers unconsciously have their feelers out all the time to determine the temperature. Is it hot or cold? Is the light yellow, red or green? Are we moving quickly today? Are we feeling overwhelmed? Are we mad? Are we happy? Are we stable? How are we today?

Thermometers lean toward their partners to determine the temperature and tone of the day. They get used to checking, not so much from co-dependency, but in a natural rhythm.

The couple's interplay, exchange and conversation take on the natural rhythm of a three-legged race. In a sense, they're tied to each other. On a short-term basis, you can find the thermostat-and-thermometer relationship between business people and clients. And you all know colleagues who can enter a room and by their mood cause an emotional wave to sweep through the office.

The thermostat in a relationship is not necessarily the one who is moody. It is usually the person who has the strongest Alpha quality, a natural dominance somehow. Barbara, who is an Organizer and Nurturer, regularly came home and found it a mess. She routinely lost her temper and scolded her family, making their evenings miserable. She learned to walk in the door with her Nurturer ability turned on and her Organizer turned off. By saying and doing things to build up her family, she created the positive environment that prompted everyone to cooperate and clean up their house.

In a family, several members can be thermostats and set the tone, but there is a natural order. One family member might set the tone for entertainment, humor and play. Another will regulate serious growth, setting goals, and achievement. It's subtle, but it's something we trip over and need to recognize with those closest to us.

Someone in the relationship always fills the neutral void. That's the thermometer's role. The thermometer always looks to stabilize the environment, seeking a comfortable temperature. Thermometer members of relationships need to recognize what factors trigger change! There is usually one major causal factor. Here are three examples: for Barbara, it's inefficiency; for Tony, lack of momentum; for Jody, it is a sense of being overwhelmed. And what is the converse of each? Efficiency, movement and peace of mind. Each person is declaring a specific need when he or she changes the environmental temperature.

I tell people with problems to look past the problem to find the source. That's the true answer for response and healing. See the bigger picture. Jody must continually have a conversation with herself on how to keep from feeling overwhelmed, on what to do when she is overwhelmed, and how to effectively communicate that she feels overwhelmed. The same applies for Barbara in coping with inefficiency and Tony for inertia. Awareness and conversation with self are means and methods to share underlying needs and frustrations.

Once you've determined which of your attributes are likely to change the temperature of your environment, you can learn to draw on your other attributes for perspective and balance. For example, after Barbara determined that her Rapid, Structural and Aesthetic attributes were affecting her family adversely, she learned to withhold them when needed and rely on her Global perspective and her Relational and Learn attributes to gain perspective.

Thermometer attributes can be Temperate or Spectrum focus, Support, or any of the Relational attributes. The thermometer's usual first reaction is to duck and cover, to run for the hills. But sometimes, if provoked, thermometers go on the attack. If you are a thermometer, you must have a conversation with yourself regarding changes in the environment. Ask yourself: What is going on? What has changed? Then identify the change, the moment and the cause. Thermostats tend to create pressure points, so try to determine the pressure point and the reason behind it. *Remember, as a thermometer, you're looking for harmony, peace of mind and stability.* You don't want hurt feelings or to be bogged down in chaos or logistical mires. Therefore, you must be aware of your own needs. If your thermostat registers upset, you feel unstable. Before you can articulate that, you must zero in on the thermostat's need. What's going on with them?

Thermometers usually end up reacting, but they can react with perspective by being proactive. Instead of saying, "I'm not in the mood to deal with you" or lashing out, you can learn to ask: "How and why are you frustrated?"

Learn to start thinking in terms of action and solutions. What can we do about it? What's the way to clear this up? You can restabilize your environment. Take action; don't merely react. Overall, it's much better to come up with a solution than to continually face the emotional turmoil.

The needs of the thermometer are not as provoking or immediate as the needs of the thermostat. The thermostat person has more hot buttons, pressure points, and immediate needs. The thermometer person's needs...safety, efficiency, momentum and peace of mind...are not as pressing. Therefore, the conversation between a thermometer and a thermostat will be consistent and ongoing. For example, it is rare for me to confront my wife with feeling overwhelmed, overloaded or hurt. By the same token, my wife initiates a lot of what we do. She's the one who suggests, "Let's get up and go jogging at 6:00 am."

This is an area of major importance when it comes to interplay in relationships. It is the fundamental principle behind interactions with a spouse, child, friend, parent or client.

I have created a chart to help clarify which attributes are most powerful in setting the temperature. See Diagram 1 on page 223)

The foremost characteristic is Specific focus. The next most influential is Rapid rhythm. The characteristics are each weighted: the higher the weight, the more powerful the attribute in setting the temperature or tone of the environment.

CHAPTER 23
AWARENESS OF YOURSELF
How You Show Up in Your World

"When a man begins to understand himself, he begins to live."
—Norvin G. McGranahan

Let's look at your life job description as a person, as a parent, as a professional, and as a creature of God. It's what you're put on this earth to do. Your life job description applies to all five areas of your life: professional, financial, personal, family & friends, and spiritual.

To help you begin to think in terms of your specific abilities, let's start with a homework assignment. This exercise will help you gain a broader picture of your patterns and put them in perspective. From the ten Families, list those four or five abilities that best and most truly describe you. List them on a sheet of paper: Nurturer, Refiner, Olympian, etc. Now answer these questions: How do these abilities positively impact your business and life? How does each negatively impact your business and life? Your answers to these questions can generate perspective and awareness because you know your life and yourself better than anyone else.

Examples of positive impact: Because I'm a Refiner, I'm always improving on what I offer my clients. Because I'm a Nurturer, I comfort and encourage my family when they're hurting or discouraged. Because I'm an Olympian, I keep going until I succeed. As a Scholar, when I'm given a project, I gladly do the background research and make sure I understand it thoroughly. My Engineer ability helps me set up the systems that make my office run smoothly.

Examples of negative impact: Because of my Nurturer ability, sometimes I take on the needs of friends unwisely and set myself up to be disappointed when they don't reciprocate. Because of my Refiner ability, I can be overly critical of my children. As an Olympian, I volunteer to take on so many challenges that I don't get the rest I need. As a Scholar, I get lost in the process of learning and do not get my work done. As an Engineer, I sometimes resist changes that would be beneficial.

People usually don't see the pattern of how they bless others. They more naturally see the pattern of their pain, the negative impact. As a Nurturer, I realize that I have created co-dependent relationships time and time again in which I have set others up to disappoint me because I didn't articulate my needs. I don't normally think about myself as warm and friendly or see that people like me because I'm a helper.

I firmly believe that once you become aware you can never go back.

Themes and Physics. Here we're not talking about managing your abilities, but simply becoming aware of what your themes and physics are.

Your Themes are what you're designed to gift others with personally and professionally as a parent, spouse, teacher, and as a contributing member of society. They're the core function of each ability. Together, your Themes make up your life job description.

What you gift others with is also what you need back from others to rejuvenate you, to fill you with enthusiasm.

Your Physics refers to the interaction of your attributes with each other. And actually, physics is the science that deals with matter and energy and how they interact. For you to have the success and significance you're designed for, you must obey the laws of physics. Your dominoes have to be lined up properly for the chain-reaction tumble to work. If you're an Aesthetic who is also Analytical and has a Structural attribute...you need to create a safe place so you can find clarity so you can create the structure you need to take action. Without safety as the first domino, none of the other dominoes are triggered. Without the second domino, clarity, movement stops because structure can't be designed properly. As a result, the other dominoes won't fall correctly, and the big finish never happens.

Awareness of your physics is important...to figure out where you're stuck and how to get unstuck. Why am I paralyzed? How am I frustrated? Where does my rage come from? Focusing on where your frustration, depression or anger originates permits you to become aware of what's not falling into place.

For example, if you spend a great deal of time thinking about things, but don't feel safe to move forward or safe in a relationship, an essential ingredient to creating movement is missing. Consequently, there will be little or no movement...and certainly no optimal movement.

Refueling your tank. This is about the importance of play. I often tell people who are Ethical or Relational, "I'd hate for you to love me the way you love yourself because you put yourself last, you disappear, you become invisible." In talking with many people, one problem consistently puzzled me: Why are people so remiss at taking care of themselves, rewarding themselves, or ensuring an environment that nourishes their enthusiasm? Many of these same people are confident and competent in most areas of their lives. So why are they terribly inept at enjoying a significant life? Over time, I began to realize that your adult self supervises your work. Your child self supervises your play.

Before the age of seven, children reason with emotion, not logic. They readily believe authority figures and can embrace false concepts. As adults, we continue to believe that many emotional rationalizations are logical. In fact, we believe they're logical to the point that we don't stop to ask, "Is it logical? Where did it come from?"

I've come to realize that, regardless of age or status, there's a quiet vulnerability within each of us. That is our inner child.

In the dialogue between the adult self and the inner child, the adult must supervise the child to assure that the child gets enough play, rest and reward. Seven-year-olds are emotionally volatile. They can be afraid, hurt, sad, pouting, angry, acting out, or violent. Most of all, they need to be parented.

Discussing the inner child, a friend said, "So, it needs to grow up!" But the childlike part of you is wonderful, and it would be a great loss if it were to grow up. Your inner child is not intended to grow up. All your life, it remains an important part of who you are. Your adult self can be irritated because the child in you has needs…it's vulnerable, insecure or slows down the adult's momentum. To create movement, your child within has to be addressed. You can negotiate when to play.

Start with the simple. Master what is childlike in you and negotiate with that. Don't try forcing it to grow up. Don't censor it or tell it to be seen and not heard. Negotiate with your child self: We'll celebrate when we accomplish this goal. When we move forward in this area, we'll take a day off. When we finish our phone calls, we'll go out to dinner.

By celebrating accomplishments, big and small, you create small islands of remembrance, little acknowledgments of positive experiences. If the adult part completely dominates to the exclusion of the inner child, I promise you that burnout either has occurred or will occur. It is the child at play in you that rejuvenates you, that refuels your enthusiasm.

Your child within helps you remember who you are, how to play, how to sit on your Creator's lap and snuggle up. If you don't embrace the seven-year-old in you, and negotiate with that child to allay fears, sadness, anger or resentment, you will not derive the enthusiasm to counteract the burnout that your adult faces on an ongoing basis. Each of us needs to have our gas tank refilled. Your inner child is in charge of putting the nozzle into the tank and filling you up. It's okay if your child self doesn't have finesse about playing your way to success and significance. What's unacceptable is your adult self not guiding your inner child to become competent and confident. That's an important key to playing, accomplishing, achieving, rejuvenating and recharging.

A well-known author and speaker works out of his home. He has a recess bell that reminds him, his wife and children that they need to take breaks. He has successfully negotiated with himself by implementing that childhood practice. For recess, he takes an afternoon siesta or plays with his children or jumps in the pool. The bell is to remind them of enjoyment, slower rhythms, and playful times. After recess, they go back to doing what they do, refreshed, building their confidence and competence. The recess bell is a clever and very powerful device. Everyone needs recess. After all, Newton discovered the profound in the simple. According to legend, it hit him on the head in the form of an apple. The concept of gravity came to him while tapping into his childlike nature, as he rested and rejuvenated under an apple tree. When was the last time you sat under a tree like a child?

Why is the entertainment industry so prevalent in today's culture? Movies, music, television, video games and computers fill our lives. Multimedia has become the modern recess bell. It allows us to stop what we're doing, create space, play, be amused, be entertained, and be engaged. Although I have a busy schedule, I always make time for my movie club because it transports me from my daily life, takes me to another place, and lets me experience a fantasy. It engages my mind in a way that is new, different and refreshing. If my nose is held to the grindstone of work without respite, I forget the enjoyment of it, lose my sense of humor and become less effective.

However, we cannot remain at recess all the time. Our lives would unravel. In brief bursts, it revives us, allowing us to return to our work with new energy. When your recess bell rings, what do you do? Do you ignore the bell and keep working?

The right fuel. The more energy you use, the more often you need to refuel. And you need quality fuel. Junk fuel allows you to get by while you keep promising yourself you'll rest, stop and play whenever there is a natural break. Or it can be the roller coaster experience. I know someone who goes into semi-retirement whenever he amasses some money. Not a safe environment to build on! It creates pressure, mostly negative, because of credit card debt and poor financial management.

When searching for the tangible and intangible rewards that fuel you, remember that your rewards are specific and unique to your design. A reward for one person may be toxic for another. What's fun for someone can be oppressive for someone else. You need to engage in play that truly nurtures your soul on a regular basis. For me, it's a movie club. For someone else, it could be sketching under a tree. For the Introspective person or the nature lover, it might be going to the mountains to experience fresh snow falling. It invigorates and rejuvenates and gives you the intangible fuel to power your significance. We each must figure out the types of play that re-energize us best.

In the book, *Winning with Integrity - Getting What You Want Without Selling Your Soul*, Leigh Steinberg writes, "This is a book about the process of negotiation - which means that this is a book about life." To me, this includes negotiating with yourself on an ongoing basis. In my life, stress means instability. When I am feeling stress and out of balance, I insulate myself with sweets. Ultimately, if I don't negotiate with myself, I then insulate with fat to avoid the feeling of free-falling or imbalance. Proper high-octane fuel for me is proteins, grains, fruits and vegetables, and the right sweets at the right time...all proactively chosen by me. Stability in my bank account, relationships, home, and business also fuels me.

Concerning your reward system, sometimes you need to stretch a little. My wife and I both like stability in our world. However, we could easily end up in a cocoon-like environment if we abandoned ourselves to it. We'd lose the creativity and growth essential for our significance. When we thought about it, we realized a lot of our friends were either Expeditious or Rapid. In a sense, our friends kidnap us from ourselves. They plan parties, dinners, movies, game nights and vacation cruises; they remind us to play in a different way. Joan and I don't plan our play, but we have cultivated relationships that help us structure our play. For example, a group of us now hold season tickets to the local theatre.

As an adult, I value my themes, but begrudge what it takes to make them function well. It's part of the physics. *To whom much is given, much is required.* It's hard to be you if you don't create an environment for your own humanity...if you don't create the greenhouse to grow the orchid that's you.

As I meet successful people, I inevitably find that there is a playful quality in them. The busy president of a large company makes sure he takes the time to play golf, do game nights with his family, and take several vacations a year. He's learned that part of his movement involves serious growth, getting results and new experiences...but it also involves play, relaxation and engaging his competitive drive in a fun way. Another successful businessman runs marathons to rejuvenate. He experiences the joy of movement as he competes in races around the country. Another couple likes to take bicycle trips through France. The heavier the responsibilities and the greater the achievements, the more they need to play...and refuel.

Consider the child in others. There are times when you're not having a conversation with the person you think you are...your boyfriend, spouse, boss or colleague. You think you're conversing with the adult part of them, but sometimes it's the child in them that's expressing their need.

I know a couple who work together running a highly successful company. The wife is dynamic, but she is almost always out of breath. There are so many shoulds in her life and too many pressure points. She reminds me of the Alice in Wonderland rabbit who ran around muttering, "I'm late, I'm late for a very important date." When I was consulting with both of them about their relationship on and off the job, I told her I wished her peace of mind. Our conversation stopped, and the husband said, "That's uncanny because for years it is the same thing that I have wished the most for her."

She never evidenced peace of mind because her adult self never had a conversation with her inner child about creating peace of mind. I encouraged him to find a picture of his wife when she was seven years old and tape it to the dashboard of his car. The photo would remind him of her inner child with whom he sometimes must deal. He has a conversation with that child when she is feeling overwhelmed, insecure, judged and criticized for not getting all her chores done…for not being the perfect little girl she thought she should be.

You can't reason with the childlike part of yourself or the child in someone else. You have to determine the emotional need, hurt, or want and allay it. Address that frustration or need. Allow for space, synergy, safety, and nurture to surround that child. The child can then feel safe to negotiate work and play. No matter who it is, despite age or position or accomplishments, you may be talking with the frustrated child within…the hurt child, the ignored child or the child who locks himself in a cupboard because that person has too many serious, heavy things to do.

You can identify and address the childlike needs of yourself and others based on specific abilities (See Diagram 3 on page 227.)

How to start moving. Movement gives us experiences and knowledge which in turn gift us with competence and confidence. Movement also gifts us with sensuous experiences, islands of remembrance, and clarity. It activates the fuel for our enthusiasm and reward system.

We all have a gatekeeper, an internal censor. It can stem from past negative nurture or from one of our abilities that has gone out of control. Your gatekeeper can undermine, stifle or paralyze you. Virtually all toxic people have become stuck in one or several areas of their life. Their Integrity attribute steals their joy. Or their excellence attribute is never satisfied. Their Aesthetic attribute may be too injured to dare or care. The Specific attribute can be overwhelmed and frozen, like a deer in the headlights. For some, permitting one or more abilities to take over or seize up has become a habit. This is the nucleus of toxic cancer. How we handle our wayward abilities determines our success, significance, creativity and growth...or our atrophy, resentment, depression, and anger.

Many times, people aren't aware of their own responsibility for staying stuck because they see a parent, institution, or spouse as the cause. Although other people may play a part, the most important role is yours. Questions to ask yourself are: Am I damning myself, and if so, how? Am I giving away my power, and if so, how? Am I over-owning guilt, and if so, how? The reasons your gatekeeper detains and censors you can be varied; the point is that you've given it the power to steal your joy and your significance. You have to learn to negotiate with yourself about any abilities that are out of control and shutting you down.

I hold onto a vivid image from the church in which I grew up. It was a fifty-foot-tall mosaic of Mary with incredible sapphire-blue eyes and with rays of light streaming from her hands. She was standing on the world with her right foot on an open Bible and her left foot on the head of a hissing snake. I was struck by the contrast of her beautiful serenity with the threatening presence of the snake underfoot. For most of us, the hissing snake is the beguiler of Adam and Eve.

The serpent's tactics remain the same, to subtly raise doubt by challenging our trust in the truth and undermining our value as humans. His subversive questions to us make for self-doubt: Are you sure you have any value? Are you sure you make a difference? Why are you so sensitive? Mary revealed an unspoken strength in the presence of the undermining snake. Like Mary, we all must stand up to a hissing snake in our lives. We need to remind ourselves of the truth about us and not heed disguised lies that undermine our growth and joy.

Every relationship is a dance...
with clients, colleagues, spouse, siblings, and
even with yourself. You need to talk about
the choreography with your dance partner.
If you plan to waltz and your partner
is ready to tango, there may be bruised toes.

Alicia, who has attended our seminars for years, is a professional victim. She constantly comes to me in tears; there is always something wrong, something that is too much for her. The last time we spoke, she was furious with her husband. He's the cause of her unhappiness. He's the reason they're not moving and growing and becoming stable. During a goal-writing session at the seminar, she was sobbing in the back of the room. The cause of her rage and tears didn't surprise me. It was her husband. Although he had come to the retreat with her, he spent most of his time hanging out in the hotel room.

During the goal-writing session, her husband had left and gone back to their room. She was furious with him for not writing his goals.

I gently confronted her. "Isn't it interesting that you're upset with him for not writing goals to the point that you're not writing your own goals?" I told her she was giving her power over to someone else, censoring herself, and deflecting her anger onto that person, rather than focusing on the part she played in this dysfunctional dance. I said, "Go back in and write a goal. If your husband catches up, that's great. If he gets left behind, that's his choice." Her tears stopped.

We can choose to get in the way of our own movement and blame others for sabotaging us. Alternatively, we can opt to get out of our own way and not permit others to sabotage us as we move forward.

Every relationship is a dance...with clients, colleagues, spouse, siblings, and even with yourself. You need to talk about the choreography with your dance partner. If you plan to waltz and your partner is ready to tango, there may be bruised toes.

When you're having conversations with yourself, with others and with your Creator, it's important to know you're in a dance. The movement of the dance requires finesse, awareness and coordination: you're watching your step, trying not to step on toes or trip, attempting to move smoothly across the floor. As they dance, literally or figuratively, many people lose themselves and don't pick up the signals. The dance requires you to be present, flexible, aware of who you are, and aware of your partner.

With practice, we become fluid in our moves. We know when to dip, when to pick up the pace, when to slow down. In the same way, we can learn to be present, to move, and to continuously inventory our environment, our relationships and what role we play in those relationships. If the dance or relationship is uncoordinated, awkward or painful, it is a sign that something is wrong.

Some of you continue to experience the long-term effects of negative nurture you received as a child. The insidious effects of this are demonstrated by the following true story.

I consult with an exceptionally bright woman who has overcome dyslexia to become a dynamic communicator and teacher. She also has the Integrity ability, Justice. When she was in second grade, her teacher told her that she was stupid. Because she looked up to the teacher as an authority figure, she allowed that statement to sink in and affect how she saw herself. Consequently, this brilliant woman developed a pattern of arguing about anything and everything to demonstrate her verbal and intellectual superiority. Even when she completely agreed with another person, the seven-year-old in her demanded to argue the point...to demonstrate that she was engaged and intellectually able. It was an unconscious attempt to justify herself, a reaction to the old tape playing in her head. In her work environment, her argumentativeness made her appear to be a nay-sayer or resistant to leadership.

As a Justice and an Olympian, she's naturally designed to gift others with values, principals and convictions and she's naturally determined and tenacious. However, she had a hard time trusting the praise of others when they told her she was intelligent. She abandoned herself to using her intellect and verbal skills for repartee, instead of managing and using them appropriately. The child inside her continued to try to prove to her second grade teacher that she was smart, a good girl, and worthy of approval.

After she became aware that she had surrendered her power to this authority figure, she was able to utilize her Olympian attribute to take her power back. The regaining of power solidified her true sense of self. She learned to bite her tongue when she was tempted to argue. Because she's learned how to manage this ability appropriately, her opinions and advice are sought by many. She's been able to focus her energy in more productive ways and to create increasing reciprocity, perspective, nurture, and integrity in her life.

The good news is that your design does not change. The better news is that you can change how you manage it, and this can dramatically impact your effectiveness and level of satisfaction with your life. My goal is to help you achieve this as we discuss in greater depth how to manage your abilities.

CHAPTER 24
MANAGING YOUR ABILITIES

"What isn't tried won't work."

—Claude McDonald

Through years of profiling individuals, I have witnessed countless transformations in peoples' lives. These transformations have often begun with pain, confusion or deep-seated frustration. By the time the process of introducing clients to themselves was completed, they were hopeful and excited about what their lives could become. The positive, frequently dramatic turn-around in people is the predictable result of becoming aware, acting on it, and growing proficient at managing their attributes.

I want you, the reader, to experience the powerful impact of utilizing your natural abilities in harmony to create a better, fuller life. I wish you to experience the personal joy of remembering who you are and the hope that comes in realizing who you were created to be.

You will encounter difficulties if you simply assume that natural law will bring success without intelligent effort on your part. If you bury your natural abilities under ignorance and apathy, you'll reap a mediocre life. The harvest will be confusion, frustration, and living in reaction to your circumstances. Now is the defining moment for you to decide to take the path toward a better you.

I am blessed to know a woman named Carolyn. She reminds me of the silent screen star, Mary Pickford...tiny in stature, but a giant of a woman. Carolyn is a wonderful combination of fragility and strength. When I first encountered her, she was in enormous personal and business debt, on the verge of losing to her circumstances. As we spoke, I emphasized that she could leverage her innate nature and utilize her strong points to overcome the many obstacles she faced. I gave her a strategy for the present and hope for the future...making it clear that she must permit herself to be human and that she needed to celebrate each and every victory, however small. Transformation is such a bigger-than-life process that at times it seems unreal. Within a few years, she was free of debt, had paid her back taxes, and was able to fund her retirement portfolio. Her life still exhibits her sweetness and fragility, but she has embraced stability and gained strength. No matter what our physical stature, we all have an inner giant that needs championing, direction and celebration.

Once you set goals that match your heart's desires and set yourself to pursue them using your new awareness, you'll be unstoppable.

I absolutely believe that, and I encourage you to take stock of where you are in your life and what you want. Take the time to reflect on it! I'm a serious advocate of taking a personal day off with no agenda...other than self-examination. Am I moving toward my natural desires and goals, or am I being derailed in my pursuit of them? Too often, people ignore or suspend personal goals while they pursue an agenda someone else has set for them. I've witnessed individuals sincerely try to thrive according to someone else's agenda for decades. The common threads for all of them have been failure to take stock of who they are and losing touch with what truly motivates them. Inventorying who you are is essential to remembering who you are. And acting on that awareness is the key to engineering your true success and significance.

Not long ago, we had a national conference with clients from 28 States. A big occasion. What I remember most about it was a comment my father made at lunch the next day. We'd been talking around the table about how blessed we were as a family to be able to help people become the best they can be. My father looked at me and said, "John you've been surrounded by what you've needed all along." Of course, Dad was right. I was surrounded by what I needed all along and so are you. You just have to look for it.

When trying to clarify complicated areas of your life, look for the specific roadblock and question it. Ask unconventional questions without an agenda other than clarity and truth. I've had much success with clients in determining the highest and best use of their time by using this simple exercise: Divide a piece of paper into four equal columns. In

Column 1, list all the tasks you do; in Column 2, using a scale from 1 to 10 with 10 being highest, mark your level of confidence and competence for each task; in Column 3, again using a scale from 1 to 10, mark your level of enjoyment for each task; in Column 4, put the total of Columns 2 and 3 for each task. Remember, enjoyment equates to rewards; rewards equate to enthusiasm; and enthusiasm equates to success. Examine what you've clarified. Use a highlighter pen to highlight anything that has a total of 14 or higher. Anything highlighted is the beginning of your new job description. These are tasks you're good at AND enjoy as well. Now, take the unhighlighted areas and figure out how you can outsource, negotiate or delegate those tasks. This exercise can be applied in any profession, from homemaker to CEO. Regardless of complexity, there are always ways to clarify and overcome the obstacles you face in life.

Discerning points of conflict. Have you ever noticed that there can be no real winner when you pick a fight with yourself? You merely frustrate and paralyze yourself. This is one type of conflict point, internal. There are at least three major kinds of conflict points:

❏ internal conflict, caused when one of your abilities clashes with another of your abilities;

❏ a clash between your abilities and the abilities of someone else;

❏ conflict that occurs when your environment clashes with your innate abilities.

Internal Conflict. Can you imagine Mother Teresa duking it out with Frank Sinatra? Well, that's what happens when Nurturer and Free Spirit attributes fight for dominance in the same person. This internal wrestling goes on continuously when it is left unresolved. That's why it's essential to begin the ability management process by establishing awareness and leveraging that newfound awareness to adjudicate the conflict. *The more aware of yourself you are, the better your self-parenting skills will be.* No one ability will always prevail. You have to develop the sophistication to decide when your Free Spirit should take the lead and when your Nurturer should take the lead.

Jeff Wilson, a client who had both Justice and Performer abilities, was frustrated by internal conflicts. Unmanaged, these two abilities cancelled each other. He desired the serious impact that his Justice ability provided and the enjoyment his Performer ability brought him. But, in a sense, they hated each other and opposed each other. His energy was being consumed by his inner battle. When I reviewed his profile, I brought him to a new level of awareness about his conflict. Jeff learned to consciously delineate between Justice and Performer. His Justice couldn't always be right, and his Performer couldn't always be validated by response...but he could harness and focus his energy to find an appropriate place for both. Recently, he participated in a 400-mile bike ride for charity. His Justice enjoyed the serious impact of raising $20,000 for charity. His Performer enjoyed being celebrated for the accomplishment. He and all those around him benefited when he used these abilities in harmony instead of in opposition to each other.

The suit of armor syndrome. To some degree, virtually everyone has what I call "the suit of armor syndrome." They appear to be wearing a titanium suit of armor from head to toe. Viewed from the front, their aura of strength seems impenetrable...but turned around, seen from the back, they're butt-naked. They're really wearing only half a suit of armor.

For example, as an Olympian and Pioneer, the person in the armor can be a strong leader. However, add the Performer attribute, and that individual can be extremely sensitive to the responsiveness of others. So you have this impressive, protective armor that people see and a vulnerable backside that most people don't see. The armored side makes others nervous or fearful or respectful. Most pretend that this vulnerability doesn't exist. This is a touchy issue. Our profiling can help you in business and life so that your strong side is respected and your sensitive side is honored and protected.

When your abilities clash with someone else's. I get many requests to review the profiles of couples together. That brings to mind Jerry and his wife Kim. When I first met with them, they'd resigned themselves to a long-standing stalemate in their marriage. They felt hopeless about finding any breakthrough or solution. They welcomed my shared insights and addressed the conflict points in their relationship, sore spots that had haunted them for thirty years. Jerry was Global and Pragmatic; Kim was Specific and Aesthetic. Historically, Kim felt invisible because Jerry lived in his own head, dreaming the big dreams. He loved her with his actions, not his words. Kim needed to be loved with his words. Jerry was frustrated. He felt he was wrestling an invisible octopus when he tried to clarify her hurt and feelings of being overwhelmed.

At their normal level of interaction at the breakfast table, Jerry would hide behind his newspaper, being globally disengaged. Meanwhile, Kim carried on a monologue from the kitchen, being specifically engaged. Jerry believed that being physically present at breakfast with his wife demonstrated his commitment to the relationship. Kim saw it as Jerry eating at a diner with a familiar waitress to whom he only gave lip service. Kim sincerely desired a shared experience of connection and intimacy. Their lack of effective interplay created a chasm between them that over the years had filled with regret, anger and resentment.

Each profile is dramatic by itself, and even more so when combined with another. During our consultation, I gave them a simple exercise...an intellectual and experiential process to help them discover the truth about themselves in relation to each other's profile. They enthusiastically accepted their assignment, not knowing what they were about to experience. The exercise was: Have a Monday morning meeting to both get on the same page and to review practical logistics which Jerry would appreciate. Kim, feeling in tune with her husband, could start her week off being acknowledged and validated. Jerry could also benefit by the hope this meeting generated. It could help him achieve his bigger-picture goals while assuaging Kim's desire to address their day-to-day problems.

A week passed, and I received an enthusiastic call from Jerry. He shared the events of their first Monday morning meeting. Jerry and Kim went out to breakfast. The main topic was Kim's upcoming trip. Jerry caringly reviewed everything he felt Kim needed for her trip...the cost of travel, spending money, total logistics. His Global attribute was proud of being able to land long enough to focus on the details. But he was in for a surprise.

When they used the "mirror-back" technique I shared with them, requiring Kim to re-state what had been discussed, she tearfully told Jerry what she'd heard. She heard him say that she was lazy, irresponsible and stupid because he took over the details, placed an emphasis on the money, and seemed to think she couldn't handle the logistics by herself.

To describe Jerry as dumbfounded would be an understatement. He suddenly comprehended the ramifications of their two different perspectives colliding. Because of our previous conversation, instead of being irritated, he re-clarified his loving intent. Kim felt reassured by the time and the obvious genuine effort he spent to validate her with his words. The experience unified them and gave them enthusiastic hope for the rest of their relationship.

When your abilities clash with someone else's, try to clarify the real issues by using the mirror-back technique. It is a terrific aid to achieving harmony in your relationships.

Conflict between your abilities and your environment. The third type of conflict occurs when our natural abilities clash with our environment. This can be dramatic or subtle. An exceptionally dynamic client approached me with a story from his past, wondering how to build from his predicament. He was an entrepreneur with the Olympian attribute and a big problem: he was bored. The problem was subtle, and he hadn't noticed it. He'd been extraordinarily successful in his industry and had mastered the challenges. Nothing new or invigorating confronted him, so he decided to become involved in a completely uncharted industry. He had no background in that area of business, and, within six months, he lost 2.5 million dollars and undermined his successful, established business irrevocably.

When I reviewed his profile, I pointed out to him that boredom plus his natural desire for challenge engineered his business failure. I also shared with him that he was designed to leverage insights and asked him what insights he could gain from this expensive lesson. He committed himself to a process of learning and applying what he learned to establish a core business while engaging in complementary challenges. He learned that, when bored, he could engage in competitive sports. This stimulated his desires for challenges and mastery without undermining his business foundation. Within a few years, he turned his 2.5 million dollar lesson into a 40 million dollar company.

The lesson is: when bored with their conveyor belt, Olympians tend to throw a wrench into the machinery to watch the pretty sparks fly. And, building from scratch is an alternative for them, but not the best alternative.

The effects of positive and negative nurture. We all have experienced both positive and negative nurture. Parents, siblings, institutions and organizations can honor, promote and champion who we are naturally designed to be or they can oppress and stifle it. Based on certain attributes and styles...especially Aesthetic, Integrity and Impress...some people are prone to give their power over to their negative nurture. It can be like trying to find their true selves in the mirrors of a carnival fun-house; they see odd and disturbing images provided by the distorting mirrors of their negative nurture. The process of over-owning negative nurture creates a liquid sense of self. Our process helps solidify people's true selves and move them toward their true significance.

Here's a painful-but-helpful question for parents to consider: Am I trying to wear my children down to get them to fulfill my agenda and to value what I value? This applies to any child of any age. For example, if you're a Justice mother with a free-spirited son, you need to accept that he will always value freedom over integrity. No amount of motivating, convincing or nagging will ever change that. Rather, it will push him away and alienate him. If the mother can manage her strong desire for Integrity and love her son the way he needs to be loved, with flexibility and freedom, he'll be more receptive to her uprightness.

Pragmatics seldom experience damage from the negative words and experiences of their nurturers. They can sometimes be damaged by the actions of others, occasionally resulting in a poor image of themselves. The Pragmatic characteristic generally mirrors and is tempered by the person's other abilities. For Pragmatics with Integrity in their profile, the negative action lingers and echoes longer within them. For Olympian Pragmatics, negative nurture might spur them to action. However, for an excellence-focused Pragmatic, it could cause ongoing humiliation.

How to manage predatory, toxic or negative-nurture situations. By now, you've probably inventoried the predators that make you toxic. Next, inventory your environments to determine if those predators exist in an active or inactive state. (See Diagram 2 on page 224.) Toxic situations such as overwhelming debt, and toxic individuals, perhaps your mother-in-law or difficult boss, can be predators. If you determine that there is significant toxicity in your environment, get ready to fight or take flight. Sometimes it's simply a matter of taking your power back. Or you may need to set up a plan to eventually remove yourself from that environment. Or you may be able to re-engineer your environment.

If you decide to leave, it's important that you're empowered and that it's not simply retreating. Learn whatever the lesson is in this. Otherwise, you'll just engineer the same circumstances and duplicate the environment over and over.

I recall that a client approached me in a severely broken state. Just about every area of her life was in upheaval. Her husband was abusive and oppressive; she was drowning in debt; and one of her children had been seriously injured. So she had a toxic individual and a toxic environment to deal with. Her circumstances were extraordinary; therefore, the homework I gave her was extensive. The first thing I addressed was the mistreatment by her husband...a core issue. He viewed her as stupid, lazy and second-best. I confronted her with the truth about herself...both her co-dependency and her strengths. She was a good business-woman who enjoyed helping people and seeing movement and growth around her. But by trying to control things that were out of her control, she had become an over-protective mother to her kids. I encouraged her to take her power back from her husband, set boundaries, and tell him, "No counseling, no marriage." She learned to inventory her movement and growth in her business and to celebrate the little victories. I also gave her some specifics on how to effectively talk to her Creator about her fear issues.

The next time I saw her, several months later, she'd lost 35 pounds, reduced her debt, and her business was thriving. She had separated from her husband, but was in counseling with him. Her sense of self was solidified. She was finally allowing herself to have fun and experience the simple joys that were there all along.

My Mom. I have to tell you about my mother who has a splendid profile. She is designed to be sensitive and nurturing, yet competitive. My Mom was born three years after the death of her sister, Sadie, who was only four years old when she died. Sadie was "a little lady", to quote my grandparents. My Mom was a tomboy. She enjoyed competing in the female version of the Gaelic game, hurling. She roller-skated until her skates broke when she was 13 years old. And she was devastated when her father gave her a ladylike watch to replace the broken roller skates.

Mom didn't learn to drive until she was fifty. She took up golf at the same age. My grandmother passed away during that period, and it was only then that my mother began to find her own voice...and to become aware of who she was designed to be. My mother now thrives by competing at her golf club, socializing with her friends, speaking to other groups, and representing the state junior girls' golf team. She now has her own car and drives wherever she wants. All this since she started growing into herself at fifty.

Mom couldn't compete with a departed sister...although she tried by apologizing for who she was and by attempting to be something she was not designed to be. My mother is a driven, heartfelt, passionate woman. She was not appreciated or validated for who she was by her mother. Although

I am sure my grandmother loved her, in her grief she always longed for the daughter she lost. The message my Mom got was that she wasn't acceptable or lovable simply for herself.

Generational sin is the passing down of bent and broken patterns or bent and broken behavior from one generation to the next. If you have been negatively affected by your nurture, you can break the pattern and experience wholeness for yourself. And you can pass on healthier patterns to your own children.

Schools, corporations, and other organizations can also honor and encourage their students, employees and members to live out their design or they can criticize and discourage them. The free-spirited, independent child and the introspective, artistic child are especially at risk. As parents, you can help your children find their voice in their environments and institutions and act as their strongest advocates.

CHAPTER 25
GOALS, MOTIVATION AND THE WAY FORWARD

"One can never consent to creep when one feels an impulse to soar."

—Helen Keller

During the goal-writing sessions at our seminars, people react in different dramatic ways. Some cry. Some excuse themselves because they're overcome with emotion. Others become so excited they can barely contain themselves. And some quietly re-ignite their fire to begin focusing on their next level of significance. The one thing you will not see is any of them looking over each other's shoulders, trying to copy their neighbor's deep-seated passions and desires. As odd as that sounds, in life we can end up doing just that by following the latest craze.

Losing weight is a goal many share, but it has to be fed by individual desire. As I began appearing more frequently in the public eye, my own desire to lose weight was spurred by the realization that I wasn't a good physical representative of my own beliefs. I'd joke with people that I had three wardrobes: big, huge and Oh my God! As with all humor, there was an element of truth in it. I was internally motivated to lose weight because I realized being overweight would lessen my credibility, dilute my message of transformation, and reduce the impact of my life's work. The heart of a true goal is revealed when we identify the "why" behind it. Why do I want this? Why is it important to me? Only a "why" can sustain me in moving toward my goal. Because I'm synergistic and gregarious, I involved several health-care professionals in my effort. Doctors, nutritionists and personal trainers provided me the expertise, consistency and accountability I needed. The other essential ingredient was time...to make sure this would be a life-style change and not some generic quick-fix.

Anything you do to transform your lifestyle requires time to take root. We impatiently want to expedite our own growth, but our innate abilities are organic. In our impatience, we may unconsciously force something unnaturally and engineer unforeseen problems.

I had to cultivate patience. It has taken me four years, three gyms, a marathon, and the consistent coaching of trained professionals to achieve a 27% body-fat loss and lose 80 pounds. When you look for quick fixes based on infomercials promising major changes in 90 days, you engineer ultimate failure. There is no easy way. When you inventory the Why, the How becomes apparent.

I noticed a trend after the goal-writing sessions at our

seminars: people approached me with frustration and embarrassment. Apologetically, they would share that they didn't get it. No bells rang. They felt left out because others around them were delighted with the passion and detail of their goals. While some people were fired up, others went away dejected.

When you inventory the Why, the How becomes apparent.

When we motivate the everyman with uniform goal-setting, we get dramatically polarized results. Creating real goals for yourself has to come from how you see your world and how you are individually motivated to move and grow. Remember, a Specific person has a lens that can vividly see the ladybug crawl across the leaf. A Global person has a telescopic lens that can see the debris in the rings of Saturn. Goal writing must be modified for each. Specific persons can describe their ideal day and week; that is, idealize their present and then project that out into the future. They then can list in detail the time, energy and resources required to make it happen.

Although Global persons have no problem visualizing a dream, they can become frustrated with the details of accomplishing that dream. They become hopeless because they feel their dream is on the other side of the Grand Canyon...visible but unreachable. When championing a Global individual to write a goal, I simply reverse the order requested of the Specific individual. Individuals with Global perspective need to start with their long-term goal and work backward, creating the series of sequential mini-goals required to get there. That way, they can sustain their hope for success. They see that what they're doing today moves them closer to their dream for the future.

Writing goals to your natural design is the best way to sustain long-term success and significance.

Truth Statements. When we interview clients, we listen for patterns revealing their core motivations. We take these patterns and turn them into what we term "truth statements". I've developed a system whereby we mirror back the truth statements to the client so the client can own them as affirmations. The truth statements are essentially reminders of who they are, what motivates them, and what direction they need to go. Next, we ask them to create detailed goals based on their truth statements.

For example, a friend of mine, Todd Nordstrom, is a Nurturer. One of his truth statements is: "I am encouraged when I make an impact on the lives of others." As he became successful financially and made progress toward achieving his health and lifestyle goals, he revisited his truth statements for next-level goals. When he came back to his core truth statement about impacting the lives of others, he established new relevant goals. On Tuesday nights, he works with an organization that provides support services for children who've been placed in protective care. He helps these kids with homework, plays with them and encourages them. One summer, he realized the children would have no new shoes, clothes or supplies for school, increasing their self-consciousness. So he established the goal of sponsoring a fundraising event in his sphere of influence. It generated thousands of dollars to help the kids and has become an annual event. It is a beautiful thing to watch someone do what they were created for and witness the impact it has on other lives.

When I hear people cry for what they desire, they can be convincing, passionate, articulate. At face value, I hear their yearning, but I look to see if there's any movement behind the passion. As I've said before, a wish is a goal without legs.

I have a creative friend, Alton Hitchcock, who is a writer, director and actor. For years, he talked about moving to Hollywood, but put no legs to his talk. Then he experienced a series of events that brought him to the end of himself. He utilized this as a pressure point to muster the do-or-die, now-or-never courage to move. He went to Hollywood, found a job that gave him time to attend classes, to network, and to join the right guilds and unions. Whether he becomes the next Hitchcock or Brando is secondary; he's pursuing his dream. And he is healthier and happier than he has ever been. He's also inspiring others to find the courage to move toward their dreams.

Most people have trouble granting themselves permission to pursue their dreams. They think of themselves as procrastinators. In reality, they're probably not. Procrastinators are usually ambivalent about reaching the goal and the quality of the end result. The majority of us are simply not natural self-starters. We need positive or negative pressure to move forward.

Writing exercise. What happens if I do not accomplish this goal? We're encouraged by our inspirational teachers to dream big. We often shroud our goals in the billowy white clouds of fantasy, almost in a *nirvana*-like bliss. In reality, we are much more motivated by negative pressure points than by positive pressure points. I love the dream of producing an inspiring book for many to read. However, the pressure point to finish the manuscript wasn't positive. It was negative. The truth is, my distributors gave me an ultimatum. There would be massive delays if I didn't meet deadlines, and the project might be scrapped. My dream needed to be couched in a worst-case scenario to pressure the perfectionist in me. I effectively negotiated with my abilities, using negative pressure points.

The awfulness of missing the opportunity to do something is often far worse than moving through the fear of doing it. It takes a tremendous amount of energy to walk through the fires of fear. It's best to first experience the fear by writing than in tangible reality. The use of writing helps people realize their fear and prepare to manage any projected roadblocks. What would happen if you didn't actualize your goal?

How would you feel? How would it impact your family, friends and colleagues? How would you view yourself? How would others perceive you?

There is enough motivation in these simple questions to move mountains. Write your answers down on paper. Writing about your life and how it relates to your environment and those around you is the mainspring of your impetus to move in the direction of your goals.

Goals in the five circles of life: the balancing act. Our world is essentially comprised of five areas, each with intake and output: Vocational, Financial, Family and Friends, Spiritual and Personal. We need to establish goals in all of these areas.

It is both stimulating and daunting to realize that we require continuous reworking and maintenance. It calls to mind the little Dutch boy and the sea wall; as soon as he plugged one hole, another leak would spring up. If we regard the five circles of life as plates to keep spinning, we can't neglect a single plate, or it will fall. Then, while we replace and respin the fallen plate, the others may fall. If we over-focus on any one area, we engineer the breakdown of other areas of our lives and knock ourselves off-balance.

While my business was going well because I put a great deal of time into it, I neglected my health to the point of obesity. So I had to learn how to handle my business AND cultivate a healthy lifestyle at the same time. After accomplishing this and enjoying it as a personal victory, I then became aware of next-level challenges, specifically in the spiritual area. That sparked my desire to impact more and more people...and give them the means to move toward the truth about themselves. Every day, no matter what, I was motivated to work on my business, work out at the gym, and get on my computer to write. The next-level perspective prompted me to consciously and deliberately *wiggle forward* by incorporating all five areas into my everyday life.

Simply being aware of how to show up in these critical life areas is the springboard to everything else. It propels us to have an ongoing conversation with ourselves; to inventory these areas and consciously move toward wholeness, balance, success and significance. It would be foolish for me to focus exclusively on one area and let the others suffer. I could publish a book and remain obese or live at the gym and never write a book. Neither would represent the balanced, highest use of my time.

One of the sweetest clients I've ever encountered was a woman who came to me sobbing. She had suffered years of frustration over her infertility; all the solutions she'd tried had failed. Of course, I told her this wasn't an area I knew much about. But the entire time she spoke, I couldn't believe how uptight and tense she was. I shared two observations with her. Firstly, I couldn't imagine any fertility method working for her in her current state because she was physiologically and psychologically frazzled. Secondly, I noted that she had all but abandoned every other area of her life. I startled her with the home-work I gave her: to work on the other areas of her life and to be intimate with her husband for the joy of it...not as part of a frantic agenda. Her husband was the first to celebrate the notice-able difference in her attitude and focus. It prompted him to examine areas of neglect in his own life. Since reclaiming herself, she has put aside her frantic drive to conceive, gained peace of mind about the fertility issue, and is investigating adoption possibilities. The pressure she feels to have a child is now appropriate, not oppressive or obsessive.

It is important to acknowledge and celebrate movement or victories in each of these key areas of your life. If you are a business person, don't fall into the trap of celebrating only business growth. If you have a quiet month or quarter, you could become disheartened over the lack of growth. Remember to celebrate family and friends, your personal progress, and the other areas as well. Rewarding yourself continues the process of awareness and momentum.

Meaningful R&R. Transformation occurs when you begin to function with your innate abilities at their best. And these new-found experiences reinforce your owning of your natural abilities.

The epidemic problem of burnout stems from people ignoring their natural reward systems. Natural rewards fuel your enthusiasm and strengthen you against burnout. They also go a long way in helping you recover from previous burnout. When it comes to work, most of us are like long-distance runners who finish one marathon only to immediately begin preparing for the next race. Whatever happened to the lap of honor celebrating the achievement and absorbing the joy of completion, excellence or victory?

Although we have mundane, generic celebrations such as TGIF happy hours or Wednesday (Hump Day) acknowledgments, these are shallow, hollow and de-motivating contrivances. Hump Day implies we don't look for any joy during our work week. And TGIF celebrations infer that the only potential for fun is the weekend. No wonder people hold their emotional breath, delaying and suspending enthusiastic pursuits, becoming disorientated and fatigued. Over time, this pattern develops into a more severe loss of perspective.

My clients have had a great deal of success by implementing the following tips:

❏ Take a day off every week, no matter what. For those who love structure it can be the same day every week. For those who like flexibility it can be any day. And don't fill this day off with Honey-Do chores…preferably none. The same goes for checking your voice mail and e-mails at the office. These things can easily destroy the rhythm and success of a personal day. A friend of mine developed a routine with his young son. He gave the son his pager to turn off and put in the trunk of the car so they could spend uninterrupted time together. Just as we take off our clothes when we retire for the night, we can find ways to tell ourselves we're shifting gears. What gear-shifting mechanism do you use?

❏ Give yourself something to look forward to during the week. A weekend ahead, book an evening with a spouse or a friend or plan time alone for yourself. Enjoy the anticipation of an upcoming fun event. Although most people appreciate spontaneity, it is hard to orchestrate good times at the last minute because of other people's busy schedules. Sports events, theatre or concerts provide a great way to relax and enjoy life. Enjoyed with close friends, they offer opportunities to surround the event with dinner and discussion. These can be the best of times, keeping you connected to friends you might not see otherwise. Consider season tickets to establish a regularity in your scheduling. Creating pre-established dates for time with yourself and loved ones is stabilizing and affirming. It allows you to be human.

❏ Celebrate professional movement and growth with personal rewards. When you inventory the milestones, victories and growth in your life, how do you celebrate them? How do you celebrate time away from your work? Effective rewards can be as simple as a bubble bath, massage or facial...or as exotic as a travel vacation, car, jewelry or new home. The size of the reward needs to be in proportion to the accomplishment. The possibilities are endless. The point is that you have to create, establish and experience those rewards as an ongoing reality in your life.

Defeating the Monster. People do not like to discuss their debt. Because most are not forthcoming about their predicament, I gently try to determine their debt status by asking: "On a scale of one to ten, ten being most oppressive, what number would you say applies to you regarding debt." Their response determines what my next step will be. If they answer high on the oppressive scale, then I begin the awareness step in this critical area. If their answer is low, either they're not willing to tell me, or they're not oppressed by it, and I go to the next level of discovery with their profile.

One of my closest friends has had an overabundance of tragedy in her life. She shared something with me that has forever changed how I see finances and made it an important area to address with clients. Of all her difficulties, she was most concerned about the debt she amassed while she was physically unable to work. She taught me that the greatest terror for people regarding finances is the loss of human dignity. That was what haunted her.

I wonder how many people harbor this secret terror? I think the majority of us are threatened by the shame of it. Human dignity is the skin we wrap our self-esteem in.

On a subconscious level, we censor our terror by not talking about our debt. When people are willing to share this area of vulnerability, I point out the insidiously corrosive effects of debt. Financial debt is a monster living in our basement. We feed the monster with parts of ourselves…our joy, focus, enthusiasm and ultimately our humanity. One of my chief concerns is to help people take back their power from this financial monster.

A good way to undermine the monster is to acknowledge your financial debt only twice a month— when you get the bill and when you pay a portion of the bill based on your debt-reduction plan. The rest of the time you live "debt free".

The monster doesn't have to be your current debt. It can be the haunting memory of a previous situation or debt from the previous generation. All can be equally toxic. The depression of the 1930s is still real in many people's minds. In this area especially, celebrate the smallest of victories. As debt is one of our principle terrors, so should overcoming it be one of our principle joys!

Movement is reinforced by a celebration of triumph. Whether you are Pragmatic or Aesthetic, you need some form of acknowledgement for moving forward. Celebration of your victories in life goes hand-in-hand with generating energy and enthusiasm for next-level growth.

Turn off the car stereo and get some gas! Passing a gas station when you're on empty is not wise, yet we do it all the time with our humanity when it cries out for the fuel of renewal. Analytical and Introspective people need to cultivate quiet times to think things through on a daily basis. Even five to ten minutes first thing in the morning can help. If you have a hectic day, drive home in silence to permit yourself to process your thoughts properly. I also suggest journaling as another way to gain clarity and perspective.

Step back and consider the OPEN-24-HOURS-A-DAY

world of convenience stores, news every hour, never-ending Late Shows, Tonight Shows, and Late, Late shows. All of our amenities and conveniences and entertainments have engineered a hidden danger. Beyond stimulation to the point of insomnia, we have altered our natural rhythm so drastically that we've given up the time to sit and think. In agrarian times, we finished the day when the sun did. We spent our evenings sitting around the fireplace, reflecting or talking.

In Ireland, we often experienced power outages. A memory I hold dear is one night when the power went out right after supper. We got out the candles and lit them, then got out a battery-operated tape recorder and put on our own variety show. The whole family participated. We ached from laughing. We delighted in the ingenuity of our fellow family members. But once the lights came on, we returned to our familiar pattern of watching television. I have observed through my clients that we turn on stimulus when we turn to TV or electronic entertainments...and we turn off creativity and perspective.

I give a homework assignment to News junkies: Go on a 24-hour fast from the News. Totally abstain, just to experience different stimuli. Listening for and to something different can heighten your creativity and open up new perspectives. The challenge is to incorporate creativity and fresh perspective so you retain a solid sense of self in the midst of all the clamoring stimuli.

Contentment and progress. How can you achieve a high level of contentment with your current circumstances while wiggling toward your goals and aspirations?

Stability is essential. Shaping an environment for your humanity without stabilizing the important areas of your world is like building a greenhouse on quicksand. And, stability is unique to each individual. I need my finances stabilized before I am willing to even look at next-level challenges, and usually I take on only one challenge at a time. My friend requires no financial security to launch into new ventures.

When we over-focus on stability, however, we can sacrifice creativity and growth to maintain the level of security we possess currently. We become unwilling to move, fearing we will lose what we have. We need to think of stability as a springboard to higher levels of success and significance. Remember, the most effective means of dealing with fear is movement.

Change is something we all resist. We each have our individual comfort zone. I regard the concept of comfort zone somewhat differently than most. I believe that people seek to become comfortable in their *discomfort zone* by trying to build around areas that they realize require attention. The child in us locks the bogeyman behind a door instead of facing him. In my own case, although many areas of my life were going well, I longed to write a book that would help others. Even though I was comfortable in my life, I felt a sense of incompleteness. The discomfort came from my unfulfilled desire to write this book. Moving toward this goal required me to step out of my routine and confront my fears, to make myself vulnerable to scrutiny and criticism. Working through a fear is not a one-time endeavor. It is a continuing conversation with ourselves as we move through painful growth and exercise our power over that fear. We must become practiced at these conversations in order to keep moving forward. We continually move on to address the next-level roadblock or fear. In the process, we become practiced enough that movement becomes a source of stabilizing confidence.

The way forward. I find that those who are best at saying No...in many articulate ways...are also the most afraid of losing their stability. One client who was stuck in almost every area of his life consistently lamented his circumstances. However, when working with me on ways to move forward, he was very verbal about why my recommendations wouldn't work and uncharacteristically silent when it came to volunteering solutions. In reality, he was secretly enjoying the security of familiar roadblocks. Even though he was uncomfortable, he opted to remain where he was.

There is an anecdote that is quite pertinent here. It's the story of a man who was caught in a flood. As he sat on the roof of his house surrounded by raging waters, he prayed to God to rescue him. A man with a canoe came by to help him. He politely declined, explaining that God would rescue him. Later, a man with a life raft offered assistance. Once again the roof-sitter refused the offer, saying that he was sure God would rescue him. As the floodwaters peaked, the stranded man saw a helicopter hovering above him. Rescuers lowered a rope, but again he refused, resolutely declaring his faith that God would save him. Later that night, he drowned. When he got to heaven, he asked God why He hadn't saved him. And God said, "I sent you a canoe, a raft and a helicopter!" I've had some clients who stayed stuck on their own roofs and hostile to a helping hand.

Another way to manage your abilities is by identifying what your abilities specifically need (See Diagram 3 on page 227.) If you're destabilized in any area(s) of your life, an effective management technique is to inject additional stability into another area to compensate, at least during the transition from instability to victory.

For example, if Frank is in debt, he may be working to generate extra income, save his money, and pay off the debt. This transpires as a process, not an event. So, during this process, Frank can become overwhelmed with fear, doubt and toxic self-conversation. What if he went to weekly church services to build up his faith or enrolled in a class on managing personal finances? Either or both would enhance his creativity, spiritual well-being, practical education, confidence and social support.

Another case in point: Sean is a gentle, caring soul, stuck in his life. He's chosen stabilizing his world over moving in his world. He lives in a basement apartment, has two part-time jobs, is in no significant relationships, and lives a lonely, unfulfilled existence. He is handsome, well-educated, hard-working and intelligent. Over the years, I've shared with him the gifts laying dormant in his profile. It's accurate to say that he purposefully refuses to unwrap and use them. The tragedy for him is that he might leave this planet without making his mark on it. The tragedy for others is that we're robbed of his potential. Stability is comforting and essential in our lives, but toxic when we make it our life's pursuit.

On the back of a burro. In America, I've noted many times how the big and brash and lionized are rewarded. I believe it's one of the reasons why America is such a potent society. However, it cuts both ways; many people feel suppressed because they believe they can only move forward in huge leaps. My clients experience a slower subtle-but-powerful shift when they learn to *wiggle forward.* They're not usually equipped to jump the Grand Canyon in a rocket-sled! Most must strap their goal to the back of a burro and carefully go down one side of the Grand Canyon and up the other. The patient way across is do-able, believable and safer. We can celebrate the small steps while leveraging time to cover a lot of ground.

We cause paralysis when we try to force our abilities and goals to make unreasonable leaps. Our burro stiffens his legs and won't budge. Analytical, Global, and Meticulous people are more likely to experience this. Paralysis compounds our censorship and sustains our hopelessness, oppression and depression. The universal treatment for paralysis is movement; what kind of movement depends on the type of paralysis. The major and most identifiable are analysis paralysis, emotional paralysis and excellence paralysis.

Analysis paralysis is simply non-movement from getting caught in your own head, over-examining and over-thinking. Thinkers and dreamers often analyze a situation over and over, looking for the absolute rather than the optimal solution. Why? The only absolutes I've ever found are truth, death and gravity. There is no such thing as an absolute parent, spouse or solution. Optimal solutions are the best you can do in real time with available resources and energy. *Learning to choose the optimal over the absolute will gift you with continual movement and next-level growth.*

Excellence paralysis comes from visualizing movement to a standard of excellence beyond yourself and your capabilities. This is in comparison to your own internal expectations and the perceived expectations of those who know you...family, friends, clients. Perfectionists and those with Integrity or Meticulous abilities can fall easy victims to this type of paralysis. The preventative begins with identifying for whom you're doing a task. If it's for yourself, relax and realize that unfinished creations must be part of your landscape. If it's for someone else, identify specifically what they need from you and serve them specifically to meet that need. The management point is: execute to their standards, not yours. Chances are they won't notice and therefore won't appreciate your extra effort...and, tragically, you'll set them up to disappoint you. The child in you can abandon itself to the fear of less-than-excellence and choose no action over possible criticism, judgment and scrutiny. That child will calm down after it goes through the mill a few times and realizes the world didn't end and its fears did not manifest.

Emotional paralysis is the quietest form. We are all familiar with the numbing, shocking paralysis that occurs when someone goes through a great trauma. A person in shock is devoid of emotion. Here, I'm referring to silent, undramatic trauma; the gradual subconscious erosion that comes from negative nurture. The repetitive historical pattern prevents us from moving forward. For example, a response-driven boy is told by a teacher that he is self-centered, and the teacher conveys disappointment in him. The boy grows up to be a man who passionately desires to perform for others, but his conflict keeps him from moving at all in the direction of his natural design. The emotions create a reaction so punishing that the person wants to avoid repeating the experience at all costs...even at the expense of burying his true self. Journaling will help to empower and re-establish true perspective, especially the left-handed journaling exercise on page 231. However, it is imperative for anyone in this situation to cultivate safe relationships where they can verbalize their feelings, share with others, clarify and experience validating perspectives. I am amazed at what people think is normal. Until they verbalize their historical experiences, they gain little awareness that their environment and nurture may have been contrary to their true design. Simply put, sharing vulnerability with a safe person can only benefit you. (See Journaling Exercises on pages 230-232.)

Keep moving. Keep celebrating. And take inventory of your life and impact. When I first attended church, I would listen to the message and automatically think of everyone in my life and how they could benefit from it. This provided me with a convenient way out for my subconscious...I didn't have to own the message for myself in my world. It is crucial to inventory your life and your impact on your world as a continuing task on your personal checklist. Take personal ownership for your life and the gifts you've been given. Reward yourself when you do this; it will make the next inventory even more enjoyable and rewarding.

MAP out your movement. MAP is an acronym for **M**ake **A**ction **P**lan. People are motivated by structure, substantive milestones, and documenting of experiences. When you write down the specific action steps required to reach a goal, you are far more likely to actualize that goal.

For example, my goal is to be fit. What type of gym do I want? What is my target date to sign up for gym membership? What am I looking for in a trainer? What is my target date to start working with a trainer? By when will I consult a nutrition doctor? How soon can I implement my new food management plan?

When you track your movements, you are subconsciously taking the goal seriously and giving more weight to the steps necessary to realize those goals. You can transform the goal from a whimsical dream to an achievable process if you create a MAP for that goal to become a reality.

The journey from survival to significance. Danny

Kaye said there's a difference between being childish and childlike. Take a childlike view of your journey while moving through it. Unfortunately, many people have a childish view of their journey. It's childish and foolish to believe that if we could win the lottery, we'd have it made. The lottery doesn't automatically guarantee success, significance and completeness. The adult part of you has to understand that your journey is multi-dimensional.

When we watch or read biographies of famous people, we are often baffled by what happens to them. Famous people can become lonely and isolated; brilliant people can do great harm to themselves. If someone has been blessed in one area of life, it doesn't automatically transfer success to the other areas. Karen Carpenter, Kurt Cobain, John Belushi, Marilyn Monroe, and many others have demonstrated that in the most dramatic way. We can learn from their glittering lives and unfortunate ends.

It's a natural part of the process to be rich in one area of your life and poor in another. The key is to be content with what is good in your life as you initiate the process of survival, stability, success and significance in a neglected part of your life. In this way, you enjoy your present circumstances while expending the energy and enthusiasm to pursue the next challenge along your journey.

Our lives are delicate, intricate and miraculous. If we decide to regard our complex journey as our schoolroom and playroom, we can be learning in one area while we enjoy success in another. Embarking on a balanced journey requires our awareness of how we move and the direction of our destination.

Be willing to glean the wisdom of others. When we try on new clothes, we stand in front of a three-way mirror. The mirror directly ahead shows us what we normally see; the two side-paneled mirrors offer us different perspectives, showing us what others see. We learn more about ourselves when we incorporate others' views.

Here's an example of how I tap into the wisdom of others. When I make a presentation, I ask trusted friends for their perspectives. One shares vivid insights with me and tells me how I impacted the audience. Another monitors my emotional output and tells me if I was passionate enough for the audience to own what I had to share. Yet another friend comments about the bigger-picture implications. I refine my message for my next speaking engagement, or for the long run, based on their comments.

Wisdom comes from gleaning what others see and applying it to our lives. Learn to utilize your own abilities to the max by tapping into and utilizing the abilities of others. It will greatly expand your opportunities for success. Think of their abilities and wisdom as a library that you can use for your betterment. And remember, others appreciate being asked for their wisdom and advice.

CHAPTER 26
IT'S A WONDERFUL LIFE

"The highest courage is to dare to appear to be what one is."

—John Lancaster Spalding

It's a Wonderful Life is my very favorite movie, the story of a man becoming aware of who he is and how he impacts all the other people in his life. Only when he comes to the end of himself is he able to stop, look and listen. C.S. Lewis talks about pain as God's megaphone to the world; and the end of ourselves as where the Creator and ultimate clarity can be found. This was true for George.

We can have a wonderful life when we remember what we were put on the planet for. For all the complexities of life, what we are asked to do is very simple. MIRROR BACK OUR CREATION TO OUR CREATOR. The process of mirroring back is to be thankful; to respect and love The One who gave us our designs and lives.

My challenge to you is to be comfortable about undertaking your unique journey. Be unapologetic with what is right about you. Be humble to seek out support in the areas you're not designed to handle. Be loving in the way you are designed to love, and be understanding of how others express their love. "Be yourself" rolls simply off the tongue, but doing it demands awareness, subtlety, finesse...and above all else, a willingness to grow.

Your homework as you undertake this journey is as follows:

❑ What are my natural gifts and abilities?
Write down your top abilities and dominant styles.

❑ How do I get the best out of those abilities?
How do my abilities positively impact my business
and life? How do they negatively impact my business
and my life when I under or overuse them? Your
answers to these questions are powerful in providing
you information on how to move forward.

❑ What are the roadblocks in the way of my
success and how can I break through them?
Inventory the five areas of your life (Vocational,
Financial, Family and Friends, Spiritual and
Personal) and identify specifically where are you
stuck. Then determine the time, energy and
resources required to grow through these
challenges.

❑ Who's championing me?
You are not designed to thrive as an island. Identify
those individuals and institutions in your life who can
champion you to move forward. If you lack championing resources, identify where you need help and
actively seek out a coach, counselor or friend to
clarify where you can go for consistent championing.

"Our destination is predetermined. It's the journey we go on that's most important," according to C.S. Lewis. There is a destination and a finite outcome to our journey. Along the way, we will make mistakes and have to make mid-course corrections. We will learn as we go...how to be who we are and how to honor that. My fervent hope is that, by my words, I've encouraged you to start your own journey.

There were two things my mother shared with us again and again as we grew up. Referring to the six of us children, she said, "No matter what, always look out for each other's back." We weren't experts in ability management, but we learned from our nurture to value and leverage the inherent, unique gifts of each family member. Instead of wearing each other down, we leaned into our abilities and learned to respect the abilities of the others. Some of us were better-looking than others, some smarter, some more competitive. But from the beginning of our lives, my parents positively reinforced to us that it didn't matter. Their championing empowered me, and it's the best gift I can offer my family, friends and readers.

The other thing my mother used to say has shaped my life: "Just be yourself, John." I'm passing it along to you.

Be yourself.

DISCOVERING YOUR AUTHENTIC SELF

Just think . . .
You're here
Not by chance but by
God's choosing.
His hand formed you and
Made you the person you are.
He compares you to no one else.
You are one of a kind.
You lack nothing that His
Grace can't give you.
He has allowed you to be here at this
Time in history to fulfill His
Special purpose for this generation.

—Author Unknown

Diagram 1. Triggers that Change the Environmental Temperature

ABILITY	WEIGHT	TRIGGER	NEED
Aesthetic	10	Criticism	Acknowledgment
Free Spirit	10	Captivity, Bondage	Freedom
Performer	10	Silence	Visibility
Pioneer	10	Loss and atrophy	Aggressive growth
Rapid	10	Being slowed	Speed
Specific	10	Feeling overwhelmed	Calm
Introspective	9	People, noise	Solitude
Olympian	8	Boredom	Mastery and boredom busters, excitement
Refiner	8	Unrealized potential	Improvement and enrichment
Justice	7.5	Being wronged	To establish truth
Finite	7	No conclusion	Closure
Motivator	7	No impact, disregard	To influence movement
Create	6.8	Monotony, repetition	New and fresh
Engineer	6.5	Arbitrariness	Order, specifications
Finalize	6	Roadblocks to completion	Closure, completion
Spectrum	6	Precariousness	Balance
Temperate	6	Instability	Stability
Strategist	5.5	Working hard, not smart	Others to carry out plans
Introspective-Relational	5	Too much noise, too little isolation	Appropriate solitude and relationship
Meticulous	5	Mistakes	Excellence
Facilitator	4	Being forced or pushed	To facilitate movement
Global	4	Lost in details	Hope
Periodic	4	Internal and external stimulation	To have a place for tasks, thoughts and feelings
Perpetual	4	Being forced to stop	Continuous movement
Pragmatic	4	Intangibles	Results
Scholar	3.5	Stupidity	Growth and knowledge
Nurturer	3	Non-reciprocation	To positively impact the human condition
Artist	2	Cold non-creativity	To realize and celebrate creativity and nuance
Execute	2	Inertia	Implementation
Gregarious	2	Isolation	Lots of people
Support	2	Change	Maintain the status quo

Diagram 2. Themes and Predators

ATTRIBUTE Family	THEME	PREDATOR
ARTIST Abstract	Creativity	Harsh, monotonous, ugly reality
REFINER Discern	Improvement and efficiency	Too much inefficiency and too little improvement
PIONEER Growth	Momentum	Steady-state positions, Inertia
PERFORMER Impress	Provoking others to react	Non-response, stoicism
OLYMPIAN Intense Competitor	Tenacity and determination	Taking on too many challenges or multiple unrelated challenges
FREE SPIRIT Intense Freedom	Liberty	Any form of bondage or captivity
JUSTICE Intense Integrity	Integrity, Convictions	Dishonesty in any form
SCHOLAR Learn	Deeper level of understanding or knowledge	Not applying what they learn. Too many or too few opportunities to learn.
NURTURER Relational	To nurture and affect lives Patient nurture	An overabundance of people situations Too many needs. Too many lives to affect. Can become worn out by sheer volume.
ENGINEER Structure	Achievement strategy: structured thoughts and actions	Arbitrary or chaotic situations. Not knowing what's required of them.
WORK STYLE	THEME	PREDATOR
Facilitator	Facilitation	Passivity
Motivator	Influence	Immobility
Strategist	Leadership	Inefficiency

Diagram 2. Themes and Predators - Continued

OPT LEARNING ENVIRONMENT	THEME	PREDATOR
Analytical	Clarity	Their own mind, which is their comfort zone
Independent	Self-sufficiency	Noise and distractions
Kinesthetic	Experiential knowledge	Purely analytical or theoretical environments Fear of making mistakes
Synergistic	Synergy	Isolation and private jobs Being involved with the wrong team
CORE NATURE	**THEME**	**PREDATOR**
Aesthetic	Nurturing Words	Environments and situations in which productivity or results are valued more than the poetic or humane. Environments promoting criticism.
Pragmatic	Results	Environments and situations that involve warm, fuzzy, non-defined goals. Environments where delivery is more important than content.
SIGNIF SOCIAL ENVIRONMENT	**THEME**	**PREDATOR**
Introspective	Independence	Jobs requiring lots of social interaction.
Introspective-Relational	Independence and relational harmony	Jobs which cause either their private world or their public world to dominate and don't allow for balance.
Gregarious	Friendliness, warmth	Isolated jobs or situations where people are present but no meaningful interaction is allowed.

Diagram 2. Themes and Predators - Continued

ENERGY	THEME	PREDATOR
Catalytic	Creative energy	Unrealized potential
Finite	Closure	Disruptions to their natural sense of closure
Periodic	Multi-tasking	Too many opportunities, hyper-engagement
Perpetual	Boundless energy	Obsessive or compulsive behavior surrounding a singular outcome

PERFORMANCE	THEME	PREDATOR
Create-Execute	Leadership	Unsupported maintenance and closure
Create-Finalize	Motivation	Unsupported implementation, lack of development and support staff
Execute-Finalize	Productivity	Unsupported initiation and lack of support staff
Execute-Support	Endurance	Unsupported initiation and closure

RHYTHM	THEME	PREDATOR
Meticulous	Excellence	Imperfection
Temperate	Stability	Critical change or instability
Expeditious	Accomplishment	Unproductive people and environments
Rapid	Effervescence, exuberance and spontaneity	Delays and details

FOCUS	THEME	PREDATOR
Specific	Vivid insight	The unforeseen urgent problem. Immediate, easy distraction.
Spectrum	Balance	Dealing with change, particularly as it affects their sense of balance.
Global	Hope and Perspective	Minutiae. Small, pressing logistical details which distract, under-mine and erode their perspective

Diagram 3. Needs of the Child Within

ATTRIBUTE Family	NEEDS OF CHILD WITHIN
ARTIST Abstract	Outlets for creative expression outside of their job. To be allowed to paint outside the lines when solving problems and establishing goals.
REFINER Discern	To learn to share their insights only when invited to do so.
PIONEER Growth	To become aware of their momentum and how it affects others. To develop multiple sources of significance in their lives.
PERFORMER Impress	To be seen and heard. To understand that not everyone is designed to respond to them. To hear praise when they do well.
OLYMPIAN Intense Competitor	Multiple challenges which are homogeneous. Help with deciding which challenges and how many to take on.
FREE SPIRIT Intense Freedom	Freedom to play their way to success.
JUSTICE Intense Integrity	To experience grace. Information. Don't engage them directly toe-to-toe or you'll engage their stubbornness. Provide them with information and let them decide.
SCHOLAR Learn	To apply their vast learning in focused ways.
NURTURER Relational	To see their impact on those around them. To learn to articulate their own needs.
ENGINEER Structure	Specific action steps to implement their ideas. Explanation of what to expect. A plan to work from.
WORK STYLE	**NEEDS OF CHILD WITHIN**
Facilitator	Environments that promote change. Action steps to follow, deadlines.
Motivator	To learn to directly articulate what they want or need.
Strategist	Others to help them carry out their plans.

Diagram 3. Needs of the Child Within - Continued

OPT LEARNING ENVIRONMENT	NEEDS OF CHILD WITHIN
Analytical	Time to process information and get back to you.
Independent	To be allowed to work independently and figure things out by themselves. Their productivity is directly related to how much space they have.
Kinesthetic	To be encouraged or allowed to learn by doing. (Beware experiential paralysis.)
Synergistic	An environment to talk out the action steps or creativity required for next-level projects.
CORE NATURE	**NEEDS OF CHILD WITHIN**
Aesthetic	Praise and positive experiences. To be comforted. Help with processing critiques by focusing on the content of a message rather than taking it personally. (Mirror back to them what's actually being critiqued and invite them to problem-solve.)
Pragmatic	Tangible results (money, awards, written goals) To celebrate their results.
SIGNIF SOCIAL ENVIRONMENT	**NEEDS OF CHILD WITHIN**
Introspective	Adequate time to be alone with their thoughts.
Introspective-Relational	A balance between social time and private time.`
Gregarious	To work and play around others. (Can become depressed if isolated for long periods of time.)
ENERGY	**NEEDS OF CHILD WITHIN**
Catalytic	Structure to help them with follow-through and maintenance.
Finite	Deadlines, milestones. Celebrating the completion of a project.
Periodic	Systems and structures for balance. Can easily be distracted.
Perpetual	Artificial stopping times (or they will work or play until exhausted.) Play time must balance their work time.

Diagram 3. Needs of the Child Within - Continued

PERFORMANCE	NEEDS OF CHILD WITHIN
Create-Execute	A system to finish and maintain what they have established.
Create-Finalize	Help in implementing what they've started and maintaining what they've finished.
Execute-Finalize	Positive pressure points to start projects Others to help maintain what's been established.
Execute-Support	Help getting started. Help getting finished. Deadlines Encouragement to be open to change.

RHYTHM	NEEDS OF CHILD WITHIN
Meticulous	To be told exactly what is required and when. Encouragement to pick up the pace when necessary and to accept the optimal rather than perfection.
Temperate	Encouragement to be creative and keep moving forward (rather than getting too comfortable in their present stability).
Expeditious	Support with handling the details (tend to make mistakes.)
Rapid	Support with handling the details. They move quickly and accomplish things; strong propensity for mistakes.

FOCUS	NEEDS OF CHILD WITHIN
Specific	Help with focusing on mid- and long- range goals and even sticking with their plan for the day. Can suffer from the tyranny of the urgent.
Spectrum	Help to investigate where they feel out of balance and create systems to support balance.
Global	Specific action steps needed to connect the here-and-now to the big picture. (Can become frustrated and disconnected with immediate concerns.)

JOURNALING

These journaling exercises are designed to provide personal, positive points of awareness.

Note: If you are currently experiencing depression or anxiety that affects your daily functioning, be sure to check with a professional counselor before starting these exercises.

Identify and write down:

❑ Five things for which you are grateful or appreciative.

❑ What you obsessed about today.

❑ The frustration that caused you to obsess.

❑ The fear that triggered your frustration.

Realize the fear. Awfulize it on paper.

What does the fear look like when played out as your worst-case scenario? Although fear is based on truth, once it is released, it separates from truth. An apprehension that initially appeared truthful and logical to you can grow in your mind until it becomes oppressive; censoring and paralyzing. When you define the fear by writing down what you are afraid will happen at worst, you confront the fear and can realize your exaggeration of it.

Use word pictures.

Visualize fear as a lion roaring around inside your heart, your head, and your soul. Confront it, and the lion becomes manageable, becoming a mouse with a megaphone.

Write a letter.

If you are negatively affected by toxic people, personally or professionally on a certain day, write an uncensored letter to that person. The uncensored, unsent letter:

❑ Clarifies – brings clarity to your situation.

❑ Detoxifies – gets it out of your system.

❑ Empowers – allows you to take your power back from that relational engagement.

This technique especially helps people who are intense or who dislike confrontation. After you have allowed yourself to vent in a safe way, you can return to your journal with a clearer head. Then, you can write down specific action steps to constructively deal with the toxic person.

Try journaling for 30 days. Do it everyday or 3-5 times per week. After you have journaled for 30 days, try this exercise targeting any historic negative nurture that was triggered by a current frustration or fear: *Left-handed Journaling:* Write letters to people in your history (parent, teacher, ex-spouse) with the hand you don't normally use to write. A letter from the vulnerable child inside you will begin to manifest.

STYLE TIPS: To make your journal more helpful to your specific profile:	
Your Optimal Learning Environment	**Journaling will help you...**
Kinesthetic	Review the movements of your day
Analytical	Gift yourself with clarity
Independent	Give yourself the necessary space to process your day
Synergistic	Brainstorm
Your Significant Communication Style	**Journaling will help you...**
Aesthetic	Experience a safe place
Pragmatic	Create substance by allowing your thoughts and feelings to become more real
Your Energy	**Journaling will help you...**
Finite	Create closure at the end of each day
Perpetual	Create an event to force closure at the end of each day
Periodic	Transition from one day to another; and provide an experience that captures the day's multi-tasking
Catalytic	Leverage at the start of each day

Suggestions For
Proceeding Beyond This Book

Some people are designed to learn and own their natural abilities only after they've had a heart-to-heart talk with us. We want to meet people where they're at. To do so, we offer a variety of services and tools for those who believe that they would benefit from such services. These include seminars, profile evaluations, individual or group consultation, and multiple levels of coaching. We also offer help with goal-setting, job descriptions, and effective relationships. We want you to enjoy the pursuit of your place, peace of mind, hope and enthusiasm. Through Ability Management, we aim to help you.

Providence Systems, Inc. offers a coaching program with genuine emphasis on personalized coaching tailored to your needs and profile.

We can be contacted as follows:

Ability Management
c/o Providence Systems, Inc.
phone: (800) 945-3485
www.abilitymanagement.com

Providence Systems, Inc.
phone: (800) 945-3485
www.providenceseminars.com

To Order Additional Copies of *Be Yourself:*
call 800-945-3485 or visit our website at:
www.abilitymanagement.com